QUOTABLE
QUOTES

READER'S DIGEST

QUOTABLE QUOTES®

WIT AND WISDOM FOR ALL OCCASIONS FROM THE WORLD'S MOST WIDELY READ MAGAZINE

Reader's Digest

The Reader's Digest Association (Canada) Ltd.
Montreal   London   Sydney

A Reader's Digest book

Sales of this book without a front cover may be unauthorized. If this book is coverless, it may have been reported to the publisher as "unsold or destroyed" and neither the author nor the publisher may have received payment for it.

Published by The Reader's Digest Association (Canada) Ltd.
215 Redfern Avenue, Westmount, Quebec H3Z 2V9

Canadian Cataloguing in Publication Data
Main entry under title:
  Reader's Digest quotable quotes

(Quips, quotes and quizzes)
Quotes compiled from Reader's Digest magazine.
ISBN 0-88850-598-1 (set)-
ISBN 0-88850-596-5
    1. Quotations, English. I. Reader's Digest Association (Canada).
    II. Title: Quotable quotes. III. Series.
    PN6083.R43   1997   082   C97-900388-1

Printed in Canada

This book is based on an American concept produced by the Reader's Digest Association, Inc. All of the extracts have previously appeared in editions of the Reader's Digest magazine.

Ideas are like rabbits. You get a couple and learn how to handle them, and pretty soon you have a dozen.

—JOHN STEINBECK

TABLE OF CONTENTS

A Note from the Editors

"The only thing sure about luck is that it will change."

That quote from Bret Harte is as appealing today as when it ran in the very first appearance of Quotable Quotes® in the May 1933 issue of *Reader's Digest.* Since then, thousands of quotes have graced the feature, delighting and inspiring generations of readers.

In a publication that prides itself on the art of condensation, the quotations in this popular collection represent the finest tradition of brevity: they package profound ideas in just a few words. In compiling this column, we search out quotes that are serious and those that are amusing. We look for provocative comments, well expressed, on universal themes. Ideal candidates can be contemporary or classic, timeless or topical, whimsical or earnest.

We cull quotes from a wide variety of sources—books, newspapers, magazines, television, radio, film, the Internet, anywhere we come across a likely thought pithily expressed. And these gems have a life span that endures long after and far beyond their appearance in the *Digest.* They can be found on refrigerator doors, sprinkled into graduation speeches, enlivening sales pitches, wherever someone thinks they can do the most good. Humourists and social commentators have thrived on them. And more than a few have made their way into a poignant eulogy.

By their very nature, Quotable Quotes beg to be repeated, whether you share them during trying times or use them to drive home a point. What you derive from Quotable Quotes is of course personal, yet these brief words can also serve as a bridge to connect people or ideas.

In Quotable Quotes you'll find the wit and wisdom of men and women from all walks of life and from all ages—from Samuel Johnson to Margaret Atwood, Pierre Elliott Trudeau to Margaret Thatcher, Mother Teresa of Calcutta to Mohandas K. Gandhi. Read what they have to say. And enjoy it!

WITHIN OURSELVES

It is only with the heart that one can see rightly; what is essential is invisible to the eye.

—Antoine de Saint-Exupéry,
The Little Prince

THE ADVANTAGE OF SOLITUDE . . .

Be able to be alone. Lose not the advantage of solitude.
—SIR THOMAS BROWNE

When we cannot bear to be alone, it means we do not properly value the only companion we will have from birth to death—ourselves.
—EDA LESHAN
in *Newsday*
(Long Island, New York)

We cannot confront solitude without moral resources.
—HONORÉ DE BALZAC
Madame de la Chanterie

The result of joining two solitudes will always be a greater solitude.
—PEDRO LUIS
Flores de Otuno

Solitude is a good place to visit but a poor place to stay.
—JOSH BILLINGS

The same fence that shuts others out shuts you in.
—BILL COPELAND

There's one thing worse than being alone: wishing you were.
—BOB STEELE

Loneliness and the feeling of being uncared for and unwanted are the greatest poverty.
—MOTHER TERESA OF CALCUTTA

Of all things that can happen to us, triumph is the most difficult to endure when we are alone. Deprived of witnesses, it shrinks at once.
—GABRIELLE ROY
La détresse et l'enchantement

Our language has wisely sensed the two sides of being alone. It has created the word "loneliness" to express the pain of being alone. And it has created the word "solitude" to express the glory of being alone.
—PAUL TILLICH
The Eternal Now

The man who goes alone can start today; but he who travels with another must wait until the other is ready.
—HENRY DAVID THOREAU

What a lovely surprise to finally discover how unlonely being alone can be.
—ELLEN BURSTYN

Man loves company—even if it is only that of a small burning candle.
—GEORG CHRISTOPH LICHTENBERG

THE RIGHT MEASURE OF HIMSELF . . .

Fortunate, indeed, is the man who takes exactly the right measure of himself and holds a just balance between what he can acquire and what he can use.

—PETER LATHAM

Integrity is not a conditional word. It doesn't blow in the wind or change with the weather. It is your inner image of yourself, and if you look in there and see a man who won't cheat, then you know he never will.

—JOHN D. MACDONALD
The Turquoise Lament

Integrity has no need of rules.

—ALBERT CAMUS

Integrity is something more than a charming sentiment to which we feel we ought to aspire. It is the only reliable and responsible connection between ourselves and the world around us.

—DAVID PUTTNAM

We get so much in the habit of wearing a disguise before others that we eventually appear disguised before ourselves.

—JIM BISHOP

We don't know who we are until we see what we can do.

—MARTHA GRIMES
Writer's Handbook

What we must decide is how we are valuable rather than how valuable we are.

—EDGAR Z. FRIEDENBERG

Our credulity is greatest concerning the things we know least about. And since we know least about ourselves, we are ready to believe all that is said about us. Hence the mysterious power of both flattery and calumny.

—ERIC HOFFER
The Passionate State of Mind

No one beneath you can offend you. No one your equal would.

—JAN L. WELLS

The superior man is distressed by the limitations of his ability; he is not distressed by the fact that men do not recognise the ability he has.

—CONFUCIUS

No man, for any considerable time, can wear one face to himself and another to the multitude without finally getting bewildered as to which may be the true.

—NATHANIEL HAWTHORNE

Maybe taking ourselves for somebody else means that we cannot bear to see ourselves as we are.

—ALBERT BRIE
Le Devoir

Until you make peace with who you are, you'll never be content with what you have.

—DORIS MORTMAN
Circles

If we have our own "why" of life, we can bear almost any "how."

—FRIEDRICH NIETZSCHE

Man shies away from nothing as from a rendezvous with himself— which makes the entertainment industry what it is.

—FRITZ MULIAR

To have doubted one's own first principles is the mark of a civilised man.

—OLIVER WENDELL HOLMES JR.

When one is out of touch with oneself, one cannot touch others.

—ANNE MORROW LINDBERGH
Gift from the Sea

Everything that irritates us about others can lead us to an understanding of ourselves.

—CARL G. JUNG
Memories, Dreams, Reflections

Fair play is primarily not blaming others for anything that is wrong with us.

—ERIC HOFFER
Working and Thinking on the Waterfront

Our opinion of people depends less upon what we see in them than upon what they make us see in ourselves.

—SARAH GRAND

One can only face in others what one can face in oneself.

—JAMES BALDWIN

I have had more trouble with myself than with any other man I have ever met!

—DWIGHT L. MOODY

People often say that this or that person has not yet found himself. But the self is not something that one finds. It is something one creates.

—THOMAS SZASZ
The Second Sin

You have to start knowing yourself so well that you begin to know other people. A piece of us is in every person we can ever meet.

—JOHN D. MACDONALD
introduction to *Night Shift*
by Stephen King

The best vision is insight.

—MALCOLM S. FORBES
in *Forbes* magazine

Men go abroad to wonder at the heights of mountains, at the huge waves of the sea, at the long courses of the rivers, at the vast compass of the ocean, at the circular motions of the stars; and they pass by themselves without wondering.

—ST. AUGUSTINE

If a man happens to find himself, he has a mansion which he can inhabit with dignity all the days of his life.

—JAMES A. MICHENER

No sooner do we think we have assembled a comfortable life than we find a piece of ourselves that has no place to fit in.

—GAIL SHEEHY

Not until we are lost do we begin to understand ourselves.

—HENRY DAVID THOREAU

You may find the worst enemy or best friend in yourself.

—ENGLISH PROVERB

Know yourself. Don't accept your dog's admiration as conclusive evidence that you are wonderful.

—ANN LANDERS

Be yourself. No one can ever tell you you're doing it wrong.

—JAMES LEO HERLIHY

Often we change jobs, friends and spouses instead of ourselves.

—AKBARALI H. JETHA
Reflections

Everybody thinks of changing humanity and nobody thinks of changing himself.

—LEO TOLSTOY

Everyone complains of his memory, and nobody complains of his judgement.

—FRANÇOIS DE LA ROCHEFOUCAULD

So Soothing to Our Self-Esteem . . .

Nothing is so soothing to our self-esteem as to find our bad traits in our forebears. It seems to absolve us.

—VAN WYCK BROOKS
From a Writer's Notebook

I don't want everyone to like me; I should think less of myself if some people did.

—HENRY JAMES

When we are confident, all we need is a little support.

—ANDRÉ LAURENDEAU
Une vie d'enfer

We may not return the affection of those who like us, but we always respect their good judgement.

—LIBBIE FUDIM

A man can stand a lot as long as he can stand himself.

—AXEL MUNTHE

Misfortunes one can endure—they come from outside; they are accidents. But to suffer for one's own faults—ah, there is the sting of life.

—OSCAR WILDE

We are all worms, but I do believe I am a glowworm.

—WINSTON CHURCHILL

The most difficult secret for a man to keep is the opinion he has of himself.

—MARCEL PAGNOL

Appearances give us more pleasure than reality, especially when they help to satisfy our egos.

—ÉMILE CHEVALIER

The ingenuities we practise in order to appear admirable to ourselves would suffice to invent the telephone twice over on a rainy summer morning.

—BRENDAN GILL

We have to learn to be our own best friends because we fall too easily into the trap of being our worst enemies.

—RODERICK THORP
Rainbow Drive

A human being's first responsibility is to shake hands with himself.

—HENRY WINKLER

If you want your children to improve, let them overhear the nice things you say about them to others.

—HAIM GINOTT

We appreciate frankness from those who like us. Frankness from others is called insolence.

—ANDRÉ MAUROIS

We probably wouldn't worry about what people think of us if we could know how seldom they do.

—OLIN MILLER

We judge ourselves by what we feel capable of doing, while others judge us by what we have already done.

—HENRY WADSWORTH LONGFELLOW

Argue for your limitations and, sure enough, they're yours.

—RICHARD BACH
Illusions

Morale is self-esteem in action.
—AVERY WEISMAN, MD

Lack of something to feel important about is almost the greatest tragedy a man may have.
—ARTHUR E. MORGAN

Once in a century a man may be ruined or made insufferable by praise. But surely once in a minute something generous dies for want of it.
—JOHN MASEFIELD

In the depth of winter I finally learned that there was in me an invincible summer.
—ALBERT CAMUS
Lyrical and Critical Essays

Self-respect is the fruit of discipline; the sense of dignity grows with the ability to say no to oneself.
—ABRAHAM JOSHUA HESCHEL

The better we feel about ourselves, the fewer times we have to knock somebody else down to feel tall.
—ODETTA

A man can't ride your back unless it's bent.
—REV. MARTIN LUTHER KING JR.

Never feel self-pity, the most destructive emotion there is.
—MILLICENT FENWICK

Self-pity in its early stages is as snug as a feather mattress. Only when it hardens does it become uncomfortable.
—MAYA ANGELOU
Gather Together in My Name

Trust yourself. You know more than you think you do.
—BENJAMIN SPOCK, MD
Baby and Child Care

IMAGINATION IS A GOOD HORSE TO CARRY YOU . . .

Imagination is a good horse to carry you over the ground—not a flying carpet to set you free from probability.
—ROBERTSON DAVIES
The Manticore

Imagination is the true magic carpet.
—NORMAN VINCENT PEALE

Imagination offers people consolation for what they cannot be, and humour for what they actually are.
—ALBERT CAMUS

The man who has no imagination has no wings.

—MUHAMMAD ALI

There are lots of people who mistake their imagination for their memory.

—JOSH BILLINGS

You can't depend on your judgement when your imagination is out of focus.

—MARK TWAIN

He who has imagination without learning has wings but no feet.

—JOSEPH JOUBERT

Imagination will often carry us to worlds that never were. But without it, we go nowhere.

—CARL SAGAN
Cosmos

Imagination is the highest kite that one can fly.

—LAUREN BACALL
Lauren Bacall, By Myself

Imagination is as good as many voyages—and much cheaper.

—GEORGE WILLIAM CURTIS

I believe in the imagination. What I cannot see is infinitely more important than what I can see.

—DUANE MICHALS
Real Dreams

The opportunities of man are limited only by his imagination. But so few have imagination that there are ten thousand fiddlers to one composer.

—CHARLES F. KETTERING

Imagination is more important than knowledge.

—ALBERT EINSTEIN

He turns not back who is bound to a star.

—LEONARDO DA VINCI

Perhaps imagination is only intelligence having fun.

—GEORGE SCIALABBA
in *Harvard* magazine

Experience is a tricky affair—the imagination and the spirit are what counts, not material circumstances.

—SISTER WENDY BECKETT
Sister Wendy's Odyssey

One of the virtues of being very young is that you don't let the facts get in the way of your imagination.

—SAM LEVENSON

If one is lucky, a solitary fantasy can totally transform one million realities.

—MAYA ANGELOU

THE BEST REASON FOR HAVING DREAMS . . .

The best reason for having dreams is that in dreams no reasons are necessary.

—Ashleigh Brilliant

There are no rules of architecture for a castle in the clouds.

—G. K. Chesterton

Hold fast to dreams
For if dreams die,
Life is a broken-winged bird
That cannot fly.

—Langston Hughes
The Dream Keeper and Other Poems

No bird soars too high if he soars with his own wings.

—William Blake

The best way to make your dreams come true is to wake up.

—J. M. Power

Nothing happens unless first a dream.

—Carl Sandburg
Slabs of the Sunburnt West

We all live under the same sky, but we don't have the same horizon.

—Konrad Adenauer

A rock pile ceases to be a rock pile the moment a single man contemplates it, bearing within him the image of a cathedral.

—Antoine de Saint-Exupéry
Flight to Arras

To fulfil a dream, to be allowed to sweat over lonely labour, to be given a chance to create, is the meat and potatoes of life. The money is the gravy.

—Bette Davis
The Lonely Life

The years forever fashion new dreams when old ones go. God pity a one-dream man!

—Robert Goddard

A man must have his dreams— memory dreams of the past and eager dreams of the future. I never want to stop reaching for new goals.

—Maurice Chevalier

Dreams and dedication are a powerful combination.

—William Longgood
Voices from the Earth

I like the dreams of the future better than the history of the past.

—Thomas Jefferson

Everything starts as somebody's daydream.

—LARRY NIVEN
Niven's Laws

Rose-coloured glasses are never made in bifocals. Nobody wants to read the small print in dreams.

—ANN LANDERS

How many of our daydreams would darken into nightmares, were there a danger of their coming true!

—LOGAN PEARSALL SMITH
Afterthoughts

Dreaming permits each and every one of us to be safely insane every night of the week.

—DR. CHARLES FISHER

ESTABLISHING GOALS IS ALL RIGHT . . .

Establishing goals is all right if you don't let them deprive you of interesting detours.

—DOUG LARSON

Discipline is remembering what you want.

—DAVID CAMPBELL

Goals are dreams with deadlines.

—DIANA SCHARF HUNT

The trouble with not having a goal is that you can spend your life running up and down the field and never scoring.

—BILL COPELAND

In the long run men hit only what they aim at.

—HENRY DAVID THOREAU

Aim at Heaven and you will get Earth thrown in. Aim at Earth and you get neither.

—C. S. LEWIS

Keep high aspirations, moderate expectations and small needs.

—H. STEIN

Goals determine what you're going to be.

—JULIUS ERVING

The trouble with our age is that it is all signposts and no destination.

—*The War Cry*

To live only for some future goal is shallow. It's the sides of the mountain that sustain life, not the top.

—ROBERT M. PIRSIG
*Zen and the Art of
Motorcycle Maintenance*

When you aim for perfection, you discover it's a moving target.

—GEORGE FISHER

Intelligence without ambition is a bird without wings.

—C. ARCHIE DANIELSON

Whoever wants to reach a distant goal must take many small steps.

—HELMUT SCHMIDT

I've always wanted to be somebody, but I see now I should have been more specific.

—LILY TOMLIN

There is nothing worse than being a doer with nothing to do.

—ELIZABETH LAYTON

THE MOST IMPORTANT THINGS IN LIFE . . .

The most important things in life aren't things.

—Quoted in bulletin of The First Christian Church of Fairfield, Illinois

Origins are of the greatest importance. We are almost reconciled to having a cold when we remember where we caught it.

—MARIE VON EBNER-ESCHENBACH

To have more, desire less.

—Table Talk

To see what is in front of one's nose requires a constant struggle.

—GEORGE ORWELL

If people concentrated on the really important things in life, there'd be a shortage of fishing poles.

—DOUG LARSON

If you can play golf and bridge as though they were games, you're just about as well adjusted as you are ever going to be.

—Manitoba Co-Operator

The only person you should ever compete with is yourself. You can't hope for a fairer match.

—TODD RUTHMAN

The great thing in this world is not so much where we stand as in what direction we are moving.

—OLIVER WENDELL HOLMES SR.

When we have provided against cold, hunger and thirst, all the rest is but vanity and excess.

—SENECA

A glimpse is not a vision. But to a man on a mountain road by night, a glimpse of the next three feet of road may matter more than a vision of the horizon.

—C. S. LEWIS

The last thing one knows is what to put first.

—BLAISE PASCAL

We need to learn to set our course by the stars, not by the lights of every passing ship.

—GEN. OMAR N. BRADLEY

What was most significant about the lunar voyage was not that men set foot on the moon but that they set eye on the earth.

—NORMAN COUSINS

The hardest thing to learn in life is which bridge to cross and which to burn.

—LAURENCE J. PETER

Take your work seriously but yourself lightly.

—C. W. METCALF

If you treat every situation as a life-and-death matter, you'll die a lot of times.

—DEAN SMITH

Do not take life too seriously. You will never get out of it alive.

—ELBERT HUBBARD

To be upset over what you don't have is to waste what you do have.

—KEN S. KEYES JR.
Handbook to Higher Consciousness

It's a funny thing about life; if you refuse to accept anything but the best, you very often get it.

—W. SOMERSET MAUGHAM

It is not the man who has too little who is poor, but the one who craves more.

—SENECA

Think big thoughts but relish small pleasures.

—H. JACKSON BROWN JR.
Life's Little Instruction Book

The pursuit of perfection often impedes improvement.

—GEORGE WILL
in *Newsweek*

One cannot collect all the beautiful shells on the beach. One can collect only a few, and they are more beautiful if they are few.

—ANNE MORROW LINDBERGH
Gift from the Sea

Look at everything as though you were seeing it either for the first or last time. Then your time on earth will be filled with glory.

—BETTY SMITH
A Tree Grows in Brooklyn

Climb up on some hill at sunrise. Everybody needs perspective once in a while, and you'll find it there.

—ROBB SAGENDORPH

The man who can't dance thinks the band is no good.

—POLISH PROVERB

Nothing is so good as it seems beforehand.

—GEORGE ELIOT
Silas Marner

In order to maintain a well-balanced perspective, the person who has a dog to worship him should also have a cat to ignore him.

—*Peterborough Examiner*

CONSCIENCE IS THAT STILL, SMALL VOICE . . .

Conscience is that still, small voice that is sometimes too loud for comfort.

—BERT MURRAY
in *The Wall Street Journal*

Conscience is a small inner voice that doesn't speak your language.

—*Merit Crossword Puzzles Plus*

The ultimate test of man's conscience may be his willingness to sacrifice something today for future generations whose words of thanks will not be heard.

—GAYLORD NELSON
in *The New York Times*

Conscience is God's presence in man.

—EMANUEL SWEDENBORG

Reason deceives us; conscience, never.

—JEAN-JACQUES ROUSSEAU

Conscience is a mother-in-law whose visit never ends.

—H. L. MENCKEN

A conscience, like a buzzing bee, can make a fellow uneasy without ever stinging him.

—*American Farm
& Home Almanac*

The one thing that doesn't abide by majority rule is a person's conscience.

—HARPER LEE
To Kill a Mockingbird

The truth of the matter is that you always know the right thing to do. The hard part is doing it.

—GEN. H. NORMAN SCHWARZKOPF

To know what is right and not to do it is the worst cowardice.

—CONFUCIUS

Self-discipline is when your conscience tells you to do something and you don't talk back.

—W. K. HOPE

In matters of conscience, the law of majority has no place.
—MOHANDAS K. GANDHI

People who wrestle with their consciences usually go for two falls out of three.
—Los Angeles Times Syndicate

There is no pillow so soft as a clear conscience.
—FRENCH PROVERB

A long habit of not thinking a thing wrong gives it a superficial appearance of being right.
—THOMAS PAINE

A lot of people mistake a short memory for a clear conscience.
—DOUG LARSON

Many people feel "guilty" about things they shouldn't feel guilty about, in order to shut out feelings of guilt about things they should feel guilty about.
—SYDNEY J. HARRIS

A good conscience is a continual Christmas.
—BENJAMIN FRANKLIN

A man cannot be comfortable without his own approval.
—MARK TWAIN

WISDOM IS THE REWARD . . .

Wisdom is the reward you get for a lifetime of listening when you'd have preferred to talk.
—DOUG LARSON

No man was ever wise by chance.
—SENECA

It requires wisdom to understand wisdom; the music is nothing if the audience is deaf.
—WALTER LIPPMANN, *A Preface to Morals*

What we do not understand we do not possess.
—JOHANN WOLFGANG VON GOETHE

One of the functions of intelligence is to take account of the dangers that come from trusting solely to the intelligence.
—LEWIS MUMFORD

What the heart knows today, the head will understand tomorrow.
—JAMES STEPHENS

Science at best is not wisdom; it is knowledge. Wisdom is knowledge tempered with judgement.
—LORD RITCHIE-CALDER

Never mistake knowledge for wisdom. One helps you make a living; the other helps you make a life.
—SANDRA CAREY

"Next time I will . . ." "From now on I will . . ." What makes me think I am wiser today than I will be tomorrow?

—Hugh Prather

There is a great difference between knowing a thing and understanding it.

—Charles Kettering with T. A. Boyd
Prophet of Progress

The day the child realises that all adults are imperfect he becomes an adolescent; the day he forgives them, he becomes an adult; the day he forgives himself he becomes wise.

—Alden Nowlan
Between Tears and Laughter

Wisdom too often never comes, and so one ought not to reject it merely because it comes late.

—Felix Frankfurter

The wise person questions himself, the fool others.

—Henri Arnold

The most manifest sign of wisdom is continued cheerfulness.

—Montaigne

The art of living consists in knowing which impulses to obey and which must be made to obey.

—Sydney J. Harris

Wisdom consists of the anticipation of consequences.

—Norman Cousins
in *Saturday Review*

Wisdom is the quality that keeps you from getting into situations where you need it.

—Doug Larson

It is only with the heart that one can see rightly; what is essential is invisible to the eye.

—Antoine de Saint-Exupéry
The Little Prince

The more a man knows, the more he forgives.

—Catherine the Great

Keep me away from the wisdom which does not cry, the philosophy which does not laugh and the greatness which does not bow before children.

—Kahlil Gibran

The best-educated human being is the one who understands most about the life in which he is placed.

—Helen Keller

Everyone is a damn fool for at least five minutes every day. Wisdom consists in not exceeding the limit.

—Elbert Hubbard

It is easier to be wise for others than for ourselves.

—ALEKSANDR I. SOLZHENITSYN
The First Circle

People far prefer happiness to wisdom, but that is like wanting to be immortal without getting older.

—SYDNEY J. HARRIS

Learning sleeps and snores in libraries, but wisdom is everywhere, wide awake, on tiptoe.

—JOSH BILLINGS

Nothing in life is to be feared. It is only to be understood.

—MARIE CURIE

Discretion is knowing how to hide that which we cannot remedy.

—SPANISH PROVERB

THE FIRST SIGN OF MATURITY . . .

The first sign of maturity is the discovery that the volume knob also turns to the left.

—"SMILE" ZINGERS in Chicago *Tribune*

Life begins as a quest of the child for the man and ends as a journey by the man to rediscover the child.

—LAURENS VAN DER POST
The Lost World of the Kalahari

A child becomes an adult when he realises he has a right not only to be right but also to be wrong.

—THOMAS SZASZ
The Second Sin

Maturity is the ability to do a job whether or not you are supervised, to carry money without spending it and to bear an injustice without wanting to get even.

—ANN LANDERS

You are not mature until you expect the unexpected.

—Chicago *Tribune*

The young man knows the rules, but the old man knows the exceptions.

—OLIVER WENDELL HOLMES SR.

You're never too old to grow up.

—SHIRLEY CONRAN
Savages

You grow up the day you have your first real laugh—at yourself.

—ETHEL BARRYMORE

Age is a high price to pay for maturity.

—TOM STOPPARD

To exist is to change, to change is to mature, to mature is to go on creating oneself endlessly.

—HENRI BERGSON

Maturity begins when we're content to feel we're right about something without feeling the necessity to prove someone else wrong.

—SYDNEY J. HARRIS

Maturity is reached the day we don't need to be lied to about anything.

—FRANK YERBY

Maturity means reacquiring the seriousness one had as a child at play.

—FRIEDRICH NIETZSCHE

Youth is when you blame all your troubles on your parents; maturity is when you learn that everything is the fault of the younger generation.

—HAROLD COFFIN

AS WE GROW OLD . . .

As we grow old, the beauty steals inward.

—RALPH WALDO EMERSON

How old would you be if you didn't know how old you was?

—SATCHEL PAIGE

Whatever a man's age may be, he can reduce it several years by putting a bright-coloured flower in his buttonhole.

—MARK TWAIN

When it comes to staying young, a mind-lift beats a face-lift any day.

—MARTY BUCELLA
in *Woman* magazine

It's easier to have the vigour of youth when you're old than the wisdom of age when you're young.

—RICHARD J. NEEDHAM
A Friend in Needham, or,
A Writer's Notebook

Adults are obsolete children.

—DR. SEUSS

We all wear masks, and the time comes when we cannot remove them without removing some of our own skin.

—ANDRÉ BERTHIAUME
Contretemps

After a certain number of years, our faces become our biographies.

—CYNTHIA OZICK
The Paris Review

The mask, given time, comes to be the face itself.

—MARGUERITE YOURCENAR
Memoirs of Hadrian

The secret of staying young is to live honestly, eat slowly and just not think about your age.

—LUCILLE BALL

If youth only knew; if age only could.

—HENRI ESTIENNE

When the problem is not so much resisting temptation as finding it, you may just be getting older.

—Los Angeles Times

The person who says youth is a state of mind invariably has more state of mind than youth.

—American Farm and Home Almanac

If you carry your childhood with you, you never become older.

—ABRAHAM SUTZKEVER

Most people say that as you get old, you have to give up things. I think you get old because you give up things.

—SEN. THEODORE FRANCIS GREEN

You don't stop laughing because you grow old; you grow old because you stop laughing.

—MICHAEL PRITCHARD

We are only young once. That is all society can stand.

—BOB BOWEN

I've always believed in the adage that the secret of eternal youth is arrested development.

—ALICE ROOSEVELT LONGWORTH

Life is a long passage, you have to learn to be young, then grow to learn to be mature and grow to learn to be old.

—LESLIE CARON
in London *Evening Standard*

Age does not protect you from love. But love, to some extent, protects you from age.

—JEANNE MOREAU

Age appears best in four things: old wood to burn, old wine to drink, old friends to trust and old authors to read.

—FRANCIS BACON

Growing up is usually so painful that people make comedies out of it to soften the memory.

—JOHN GREENWALD

Old age lives minutes slowly, hours quickly; childhood chews hours and swallows minutes.

—MALCOLM DE CHAZAL

To be seventy years young is sometimes far more cheerful and hopeful than to be forty years old.

—OLIVER WENDELL HOLMES SR.

Just remember, when you're over the hill, you begin to pick up speed.

—CHARLES SCHULZ

It is middle age that laughs, since it is difficult to laugh at the world until you have first learned to laugh at yourself.

—W. Somerset Maugham
Marriages Are Made in Heaven

There is always some specific moment when we become aware that our youth is gone; but, years after, we know it was much later.

—Mignon McLaughlin

It takes about ten years to get used to how old you are.

—Quoted by Raymond A. Michel
in *The Leaf*

Middle age is the time when a man is always thinking that in a week or two he will feel just as good as ever.

—Don Marquis

Middle age is the awkward period when Father Time starts catching up with Mother Nature.

—Harold Coffin

Middle age is when you begin to wonder who put the quicksand into the hourglass of time.

—*The Orben Comedy Letter*

Midlife crisis is that moment when you realise your children and your clothes are about the same age.

—Bill Tammeus
in Kansas City *Star*

Youth is when you're allowed to stay up late on New Year's Eve. Middle age is when you're forced to.

—Bill Vaughn

What most persons consider as virtue, after the age of 40 is simply a loss of energy.

—Voltaire

Old people who shine from inside look 10 to 20 years younger.

—Dolly Parton
in *Ladies' Home Journal*

I have no romantic feelings about age. Either you are interesting at any age or you are not. There is nothing particularly interesting about being old—or being young, for that matter.

—Katharine Hepburn

Old age is having too much room in the house and not enough in the medicine cabinet.

—*Orben's Current Comedy*

When grace is joined with wrinkles, it is adorable. There is an unspeakable dawn in happy old age.

—Victor Hugo

A young boy is a theory; an old man is a fact.

—Ed Howe

Never lose sight of the fact that old age needs so little but needs that little so much.

—MARGARET WILLOUR

The older I grow the more I distrust the familiar doctrine that age brings wisdom.

—H. L. MENCKEN
Prejudices

Wisdom doesn't necessarily come with age. Sometimes age just shows up all by itself.

—TOM WILSON

You can judge your age by the amount of pain you feel when you come in contact with a new idea.

—JOHN NUVEEN

Sometimes the child in one behaves a certain way and the rest of oneself follows behind, slowly shaking its head.

—JAMES E. SHAPIRO
Meditations from the Breakdown Lane

The best thing about being young is, if you had to do it all over again, you would still have time.

—SANDRA CLARKE

If life were just, we would be born old and achieve youth about the time we'd saved enough to enjoy it.

—JIM FIEBIG

Everybody has been young before, but not everybody has been old before.

—AFRICAN PROVERB

You will stay young as long as you learn, form new habits and don't mind being contradicted.

—MARIE VON EBNER-ESCHENBACH

You are young at any age if you are planning for tomorrow.

—*The Sword of the Lord*

A grown-up is a child with layers on.

—WOODY HARRELSON

When people tell you how young you look, they are also telling you how old you are.

—CARY GRANT

To age with dignity and with courage cuts close to what it is to be a man.

—ROGER KAHN

I speak truth, not so much as I would, but as much as I dare; and I dare a little the more, as I grow older.

—MONTAIGNE

The older you get, the more important it is not to act your age.

—ASHLEIGH BRILLIANT

The trick is growing up without growing old.

—CASEY STENGEL

Growing older is not upsetting; being perceived as old is.

—KENNY ROGERS

The trouble with class reunions is that old flames have become even older.

—DOUG LARSON

A person is always startled when he hears himself seriously called an old man for the first time.

—OLIVER WENDELL HOLMES SR.

After thirty, a body has a mind of its own.

—BETTE MIDLER

We grow neither better nor worse as we grow old, but more like ourselves.

—MAY LAMBERTON BECKER

The best thing about growing older is that it takes such a long time.

—WALTERS KEMP

One advantage in growing older is that you can stand for more and fall for less.

—MONTA CRANE

The best birthdays of all are those that haven't arrived yet.

—ROBERT ORBEN

The older I grow, the more I listen to people who don't talk much.

—GERMAIN G. GLIDDEN

We've put more effort into helping folks reach old age than into helping them enjoy it.

—FRANK A. CLARK

MEMORY IS THE DIARY . . .

Memory is the diary we all carry about with us.

—OSCAR WILDE

Count reminiscences like money.

—CARL SANDBURG

It's surprising how much of memory is built around things unnoticed at the time.

—BARBARA KINGSOLVER
Animal Dreams

We do not remember days; we remember moments.

—CESARE PAVESE
The Burning Brand

The moment may be temporary, but the memory is forever.

—BUD MEYER

Don't brood on what's past, but never forget it either.

—THOMAS H. RADDALL

Recall it as often as you wish, a happy memory never wears out.

—LIBBIE FUDIM

Each of us is the accumulation of our memories.

—ALAN LOY MCGINNIS
The Romance Factor

One form of loneliness is to have a memory and no one to share it with.

—PHYLLIS ROSE
in *Hers: Through Women's Eyes*

Memories are the key not to the past, but to the future.

—CORRIE TEN BOOM WITH
JOHN AND ELIZABETH SHERRILL
The Hiding Place

May you look back on the past with as much pleasure as you look forward to the future.

—Quoted by PAUL DICKSON in *Toasts*

Keep some souvenirs of your past, or how will you ever prove it wasn't all a dream?

—ASHLEIGH BRILLIANT

To live without a memory is to live alone.

—GILLES MARCOTTE

There is no fence or hedge round time that has gone. You can go back and have what you like if you remember it well enough.

—RICHARD LLEWELLYN
How Green Was My Valley

Everybody needs his memories. They keep the wolf of insignificance from the door.

—SAUL BELLOW

Each day of our lives we make deposits in the memory banks of our children.

—CHARLES R. SWINDOLL
The Strong Family

You never know when you're making a memory.

—RICKIE LEE JONES
"Young Blood"

Our memories are card indexes—consulted, and then put back in disorder, by authorities whom we do not control.

—CYRIL CONNOLLY

What is memory? Not a storehouse, not a trunk in the attic, but an instrument that constantly refines the past into a narrative, accessible and acceptable to oneself.

—STANLEY KAUFFMANN
The New Republic

Memory is a child walking along a seashore. You never can tell what small pebble it will pick up and store away among its treasured things.

—PIERCE HARRIS
Atlanta Journal

I'm always fascinated by the way memory diffuses fact.

—DIANE SAWYER
in *TV Guide*

When I was younger, I could remember anything, whether it had happened or not.

—MARK TWAIN

You can close your eyes to reality but not to memories.

—STANISLAW J. LEC
Unkempt Thoughts

There are times when forgetting can be just as important as remembering—and even more difficult.

—HARRY AND JOAN MIER
Happiness Begins Before Breakfast

Remembering is a dream that comes in waves.

—HELGA SANDBUR
". . . Where Love Begins"

Memory is a complicated thing, a relative to truth, but not its twin.

—BARBARA KINGSOLVER
Animal Dreams

Recollection is the only paradise from which we cannot be turned out.

—JEAN PAUL RICHTER

The true tomb of the dead is the heart of the living.

—JEAN COCTEAU

There is something terrible yet soothing about returning to a place where you once lived. You are one of your own memories.

—MARY MORRIS
Crossroads

Some folks never exaggerate— they just remember big.

—AUDREY SNEAD

The older a man gets, the farther he had to walk to school as a boy.

—*Commercial Appeal*
(Danville, Virginia)

There are three things I always forget: names, faces and . . . I can't remember the other.

—ITALO SVEVO,
quoted in *The "Quote . . . Unquote"
Book of Love, Death and the Universe*

No memory is ever alone; it's at the end of a trail of memories, a dozen trails that each have their own associations.

—LOUIS L'AMOUR
Ride the River

THINGS AIN'T WHAT THEY USED TO BE . . .

Things ain't what they used to be and probably never was.

—WILL ROGERS

We have all got our "good old days" tucked away inside our hearts, and we return to them in dreams like cats to favourite armchairs.

—BRIAN CARTER
Where the Dream Begins

Nostalgia is a file that removes the rough edges from the good old days.

—DOUG LARSON

In the old days, when things got rough, what you did was without.

—BILL COPELAND

Nostalgia is like a grammar lesson: you find the present tense and the past perfect.

—*The United Church Observer*

The past should be a springboard, not a hammock.

—IVERN BALL

The essence of nostalgia is an awareness that what has been will never be again.

—MILTON S. EISENHOWER
The Wine Is Bitter

There has never been an age that did not applaud the past and lament the present.

—LILLIAN EICHLER WATSON
Light from Many Lamps

Each generation imagines itself to be more intelligent than the one that went before it, and wiser than the one that comes after it.

—GEORGE ORWELL

Nothing seems to go as far as it did. Even nostalgia doesn't reach back as far as it used to.

—*Changing Times*

You can clutch the past so tightly to your chest that it leaves your arms too full to embrace the present.

—JAN GLIDEWELL
in St. Petersburg *Times*

I don't like change. Same old house, same old wife, same old kids, same old dogs—they're on their fourth or fifth generation now. I even had the same car, a Mercedes, for fifteen years until it died of rust.

—FRANK MUIR
in *The Daily Telegraph*

The older you get, the greater you were.

—LEE GROSSCUP

PEOPLE TOGETHER

> It's the things in common that make relationships enjoyable, but it's the little differences that make them interesting.
>
> —TODD RUTHMAN

HOME IS A PLACE . . .

Home is a place you grow up wanting to leave, and grow old wanting to get back to.

—JOHN ED PEARCE
in Louisville *Courier-Journal Magazine*

The fireside is the tulip bed of a winter day.

—PERSIAN PROVERB

The home is not the one tame place in the world of adventure. It is the one wild place in the world of rules and set tasks.

—G. K. CHESTERTON

One of the oldest human needs is having someone to wonder where you are when you don't come home at night.

—MARGARET MEAD

The strength of a nation derives from the integrity of the home.

—CONFUCIUS

Where we love is home—home that our feet may leave, but not our hearts.

—OLIVER WENDELL HOLMES SR.

When you finally go back to your old hometown, you find it wasn't the old home you missed but your childhood.

—SAM EWING
in *National Enquirer*

Where is home? Home is where the heart can laugh without shyness. Home is where the heart's tears can dry at their own pace.

—VERNON G. BAKER
in *Courant* (Hartford, Connecticut)

A small town is a place where there is little to see or do, but what you hear makes up for it.

—IVERN BALL

My home is here. I feel just as at home overseas, but I think my roots are here and my language is here and my rage is here and my hope is here. You know where your home is because you've been there long enough. You know all the peculiarities of the people around you, because you are one of them. And naturally, memories are the most important. Your home is where your favourite memories are.

—PIETER-DIRK UYS

The reality of any place is what its people remember of it.

—CHARLES KURALT
North Carolina Is My Home

A small town is a place where everyone knows whose cheque is good and whose husband is not.

—SID ASCHER

A place is yours when you know where all the roads go.

—Quoted by STEPHEN KING
in *Down East*

There's nothing people like better than being asked an easy question. For some reason, we're flattered when a stranger asks us where Maple Street is in our hometown and we can tell him.

—ANDREW A. ROONEY
And More by Andy Rooney

A man travels the world over in search of what he needs and returns home to find it.

—GEORGE MOORE

Visitors should behave in such a way that the host and hostess feel at home.

—J. S. FARYNSKI

A TRUE FRIEND . . .

A true friend is one who overlooks your failures and tolerates your successes.

—DOUG LARSON

One does not make friends. One recognises them.

—GARTH HENRICHS

In prosperity, our friends know us; in adversity, we know our friends.

—JOHN CHURTON COLLINS

Strangers are friends that you have yet to meet.

—ROBERTA LIEBERMAN

Lots of people want to ride with you in the limo, but what you want is someone who will take the bus with you when the limo breaks down.

—OPRAH WINFREY

It may be true that a touch of indifference is the safest foundation on which to build a lasting and delicate friendship.

—W. ROBERTSON NICOLL
People and Books

Getting people to like you is only the other side of liking them.

—NORMAN VINCENT PEALE

It's the things in common that make relationships enjoyable, but it's the little differences that make them interesting.

—TODD RUTHMAN

The only way to have a friend is to be one.

—RALPH WALDO EMERSON

Be slow in choosing a friend,
slower in changing.

—BENJAMIN FRANKLIN

Don't make friends who are
comfortable to be with. Make
friends who will force you to
lever yourself up.

—THOMAS J. WATSON SR.

The bird a nest, the spider a web,
man friendship.

—WILLIAM BLAKE

True friendship is a plant of slow
growth.

—GEORGE WASHINGTON

It takes a long time to grow an
old friend.

—JOHN LEONARD
in *Friends and Friends of Friends* by
Bernard Pierre Wolff

The most called-upon prerequisite
of a friend is an accessible ear.

—MAYA ANGELOU
The Heart of a Woman

You can make more friends
in a month by being interested
in them than in ten years by
trying to get them interested
in you.

—CHARLES L. ALLEN
Roads to Radiant Living

Men kick friendship around like
a football, but it doesn't seem to
crack. Women treat it like glass
and it goes to pieces.

—ANNE MORROW LINDBERGH

Could we see when and where
we are to meet again, we would
be more tender when we bid our
friends goodbye.

—MARIE LOUISE DE LA RAMÉE

Friends are relatives you make for
yourself.

—EUSTACHE DESCHAMPS

The golden rule of friendship is to
listen to others as you would have
them listen to you.

—DAVID AUGSBURGER

We need old friends to help us
grow old and new friends to help
us stay young.

—LETTY COTTIN POGREBIN
Among Friends

If you want an accounting of your
worth, count your friends.

—MERRY BROWNE
in *National Enquirer*

My friends are my estate. Forgive
me then the avarice to hoard
them!

—EMILY DICKINSON

Friendship is a single soul
dwelling in two bodies.

—ARISTOTLE

In my friend, I find a second self.

—ISABEL NORTON

No man is the whole of himself;
his friends are the rest of him.

—HARRY EMERSON FOSDICK

Friendships multiply joys and
divide griefs.

—H. G. BOHN

A friend is someone you can do
nothing with, and enjoy it.

—*The Optimist Magazine*

We cherish our friends not for
their ability to amuse us, but for
our ability to amuse them.

—EVELYN WAUGH

A loyal friend laughs at your jokes
when they're not so good, and
sympathises with your problems
when they're not so bad.

—ARNOLD H. GLASOW
in *The Wall Street Journal*

How rare and wonderful is that
flash of a moment when we
realise we have discovered
a friend.

—WILLIAM ROTSLER

A friend hears the song in my
heart and sings it to me when my
memory fails.

—*Pioneer Girls Leaders' Handbook*

To a friend's house, the road is
never long.

—ANONYMOUS

True friendship is like
phosphorescence—it glows best
when the world around you
goes dark.

—DENISE MARTIN

The proper office of a friend is to
side with you when you are in the
wrong. Nearly anybody will side
with you when you are right.

—MARK TWAIN

A true friend never gets in your
way unless you happen to be
going down.

—ARNOLD H. GLASOW

It is important for our friends to
believe that we are unreservedly
frank with them, and important to
friendship that we are not.

—MIGNON MCLAUGHLIN
The Neurotic's Notebook

The surest way to lose a friend
is to tell him something for his
own good.

—SID ASCHER

If it's painful for you to criticise your friends, you're safe in doing it; if you take the slightest pleasure in it, that's the time to hold your tongue.

—ALICE DUER MILLER

Only your real friends will tell you when your face is dirty.

—SICILIAN PROVERB

A friend is a lot of things, but a critic he isn't.

—BERN WILLIAMS

A friend is someone who can see through you and still enjoys the show.

—Farmer's Almanac

Friends are those rare people who ask how we are and then wait to hear the answer.

—ED CUNNINGHAM

The most beautiful discovery true friends make is that they can grow separately without growing apart.

—ELISABETH FOLEY

Some of the most rewarding and beautiful moments of a friendship happen in the unforeseen open spaces between planned activities. It is important that you allow these spaces to exist.

—CHRISTINE LEEFELDT AND ERNEST CALLENBACH
The Art of Friendship

We love those who know the worst of us and don't turn their faces away.

—WALKER PERCY
Love in the Ruins

No man can be called friendless when he has God and the companionship of good books.

—ELIZABETH BARRETT BROWNING

An enemy who tells the truth contributes infinitely more to our improvement than a friend who deludes us.

—LOUIS-N. FORTIN
Pensées, Proverbes, Maximes

It pays to know the enemy—not least because at some time you may have the opportunity to turn him into a friend.

—MARGARET THATCHER
Downing Street Years

Pay attention to your enemies, for they are the first to discover your mistakes.

—ANTISTHENES

A friend is someone who makes me feel totally acceptable.

—ENE RIISNA

The best mirror is a friend's eye.

—GAELIC PROVERB

THE BEST HELPING HAND . . .

Sometimes the best helping hand you can get is a good, firm push.
—JOANN THOMAS

What do we live for if it is not to make life less difficult for each other?
—GEORGE ELIOT

Whoever is spared personal pain must feel himself called to help in diminishing the pain of others.
—ALBERT SCHWEITZER
Memoirs of Childhood and Youth

Be not forgetful to entertain strangers: for thereby some have entertained angels unawares.
—Hebrews 13:2

No one is useless in this world who lightens the burden of it for anyone else.
—CHARLES DICKENS

Great opportunities to help others seldom come, but small ones surround us every day.
—SALLY KOCH
in *Wisconsin*

He is not an honest man who has burned his tongue and does not tell the company that the soup is hot.
—YUGOSLAV PROVERB

We ourselves feel that what we are doing is just a drop in the ocean. But the ocean would be less because of that missing drop.
—MOTHER TERESA OF CALCUTTA

It is well to give when asked, but it is better to give unasked, through understanding.
—KAHLIL GIBRAN
The Prophet

He who helps early helps twice.
—TADEUSZ MAZOWIECKI

Expect people to be better than they are; it helps them to become better. But don't be disappointed when they are not; it helps them to keep trying.
—MERRY BROWNE
in *National Enquirer*

You may give gifts without caring—but you can't care without giving.
—FRANK A. CLARK

Never hesitate to hold out your hand; never hesitate to accept the outstretched hand of another.
—POPE JOHN XXIII

It is one of the beautiful compensations of this life that no one can sincerely try to help another without helping himself.
—CHARLES DUDLEY WARNER

I have always held firmly to the thought that each one of us can do a little to bring some portion of misery to an end.

—ALBERT SCHWEITZER

We love those people who give with humility, or who accept with ease.

—FREYA STARK
Perseus in the Wind

Basically, the only thing we need is a hand that rests on our own, that wishes it well, that sometimes guides us.

—HECTOR BIANCIOTTI
Sans la Miséricorde du Christ

Extending your hand is extending yourself.

—ROD McKUEN
Book of Days

The miracle is this—the more we share, the more we have.

—LEONARD NIMOY

To ease another's heartache is to forget one's own.

—ABRAHAM LINCOLN

The more sympathy you give, the less you need.

—MALCOLM S. FORBES
in Forbes magazine

Honesty is stronger medicine than sympathy, which may console but often conceals.

—GRETEL EHRLICH

Correction does much, but encouragement does more.

—JOHANN WOLFGANG VON GOETHE

Money-giving is a good criterion of a person's mental health. Generous people are rarely mentally ill people.

—DR. KARL MENNINGER

The impersonal hand of government can never replace the helping hand of a neighbour.

—HUBERT H. HUMPHREY

You can't get rid of poverty by giving people money.

—P. J. O'ROURKE
A Parliament of Whores

We'd all like a reputation for generosity, and we'd all like to buy it cheap.

—MIGNON McLAUGHLIN

The greatest pleasure I know is to do a good action by stealth and have it found out by accident.

—CHARLES LAMB

Real charity doesn't care if it's
tax-deductible or not.
—DAN BENNETT

Criticism, like rain, should be
gentle enough to nourish a man's
growth without destroying his roots.
—FRANK A. CLARK

Nobody wants constructive
criticism. It's all we can do to put
up with constructive praise.
—MIGNON MCLAUGHLIN

The greatest good you can do
for another is not just to share
your riches but to reveal to him
his own.
—BENJAMIN DISRAELI

The pleasure we derive from
doing favours is partly in the
feeling it gives us that we are not
altogether worthless.
—ERIC HOFFER

Deceiving someone for his own
good is a responsibility that
should be shouldered only by
the gods.
—HENRY S. HASKINS

Life's unfairness is not irrevocable;
we can help balance the scales for
others, if not always for ourselves.
—HUBERT H. HUMPHREY

We ought to be careful not to do
for a fellow what we only
intended to help him do.
—FRANK A. CLARK

The more help a person has in his
garden, the less it belongs to him.
—WILLIAM H. DAVIS

The difference between a helping
hand and an outstretched palm is
a twist of the wrist.
—LAURENCE LEAMER
King of the Night

Few things help an individual
more than to place responsibility
upon him and to let him know
that you trust him.
—BOOKER T. WASHINGTON

Do not free a camel of the burden
of his hump; you may be freeing
him from being a camel.
—G. K. CHESTERTON

No matter what accomplishments
you achieve, somebody helps you.
—ALTHEA GIBSON

Do not commit the error, common
among the young, of assuming
that if you cannot save the whole
of mankind you have failed.
—JAN DE HARTOG
The Lamb's War

If you can't feed a hundred
people, then feed just one.
—MOTHER TERESA OF CALCUTTA

From what we get, we can make
a living; what we give, however,
makes a life.
—ARTHUR ASHE
Days of Grace

No person was ever honoured for
what he received. Honour has
been the reward for what he gave.
—CALVIN COOLIDGE

The dead take to the grave,
clutched in their hands, only what
they have given away.
—DEWITT WALLACE

The only things we ever keep are
what we give away.
—LOUIS GINSBERG
The Everlasting Minute and Other Lyrics

The fragrance always stays in the
hand that gives the rose.
—HADA BEJAR

LOVE DOESN'T JUST SIT
THERE . . .

Love doesn't just sit there, like a
stone; it has to be made, like
bread, remade all the time, made
new.
—URSULA K. LEGUIN
The Lathe of Heaven

In our life there is a single colour,
as on an artist's palette, which
provides the meaning of life and
art. It is the colour of love.
—MARC CHAGALL
Chagall

True love begins when nothing is
looked for in return.
—ANTOINE DE SAINT-EXUPÉRY
The Wisdom of the Sands

At the touch of love, everyone
becomes a poet.
—PLATO

This is the true measure of love:
when we believe that we alone
can love, that no one could ever
have loved so before us, and that
no one will ever love in the same
way after us.
—JOHANN WOLFGANG VON GOETHE

Love does not consist in gazing
at each other, but in looking
outward together in the same
direction.
—ANTOINE DE SAINT-EXUPÉRY

Why is it that the most unoriginal
thing we can say to one another is
still the thing we long to hear? "I
love you" is always a quotation,
yet when we say it we speak like
savages who have found three
words and worship them.
—JEANETTE WINTERSON
Written on the Body

Only discretion allows intimacy, which depends on shared reticence, on what is not said—unsolvable things that would leave the other person ill at ease.

—HECTOR BIANCIOTTI
Sans la Miséricorde du Christ

We don't believe in rheumatism and true love until after the first attack.

—MARIE VON EBNER-ESCHENBACH

As soon go kindle fire with snow, as seek to quench the fire of love with words.

—WILLIAM SHAKESPEARE

I kissed my first woman and smoked my first cigarette on the same day. I have never had time for tobacco since.

—ARTURO TOSCANINI

All our loves are first loves.

—SUSAN FROMBERG
Schaeffer, Mainland

Two things only a man cannot hide: that he is drunk and that he is in love.

—ANTIPHANES

Is it not strange that love, so fickle, is ranked above friendship, almost always so worthy?

—GABRIELLE ROY
La détresse et l'enchantement

Love is a game that two can play and both win.

—EVA GABOR

The giving of love is an education in itself.

—ELEANOR ROOSEVELT

We can do no great things, only small things with great love.

—MOTHER TERESA OF CALCUTTA

So many catastrophes in love are only accidents of egotism.

—HECTOR BIANCIOTTI
Sans la Miséricorde du Christ

Sometimes I wonder if men and women really suit each other. Perhaps they should live next door and just visit now and then.

—KATHARINE HEPBURN

You can't put a price tag on love, but you can on all its accessories.

—MELANIE CLARK

It is possible that blondes also prefer gentlemen.

—MAMIE VAN DOREN

Love is like quicksilver in the hand. Leave the fingers open, and it stays. Clutch it, and it darts away.

—DOROTHY PARKER

In true love the smallest distance is too great, and the greatest distance can be bridged.
—HANS NOUWENS

Only love can be divided endlessly and still not diminish.
—ANNE MORROW LINDBERGH

Love and time—those are the only two things in all the world and all of life that cannot be bought, but only spent.
—GARY JENNINGS
Aztec

It's easy to halve the potato where there's love.
—IRISH PROVERB

So long as we love we serve; so long as we are loved by others, I would almost say that we are indispensable.
—ROBERT LOUIS STEVENSON

The best proof of love is trust.
—JOYCE BROTHERS

Love is proud of itself. It leaks out of us even with the tightest security.
—MERRIT MALLOY
Things I Meant to Say to You When We Were Old

Love is a great beautifier.
—LOUISA MAY ALCOTT

Let there be spaces in your togetherness / And let the winds of the heavens dance between you.
—KAHLIL GIBRAN

Familiarity, truly cultivated, can breed love.
—JOYCE BROTHERS

Love is what you've been through with somebody.
—Quoted by JAMES THURBER
in *Life*

Love is a fruit in season at all times, and within the reach of every hand.
—MOTHER TERESA OF CALCUTTA

Love is an image of God, and not a lifeless image, but the living essence of the all-divine nature which beams full of all goodness.
—MARTIN LUTHER

Where there is great love, there are always miracles.
—WILLA CATHER
Death Comes for the Archbishop

The Bible tells us to love our neighbours, and also to love our enemies; probably because they are generally the same people.
—G. K. CHESTERTON

No disguise can long conceal love where it is, nor feign it where it is not.

—FRANÇOIS DE LA ROCHEFOUCAULD

We are shaped and fashioned by what we love.

—JOHANN WOLFGANG VON GOETHE

Him that I love, I wish to be free—even from me.

—ANNE MORROW LINDBERGH

No one worth possessing can be quite possessed.

—SARA TEASDALE

The ultimate test of a relationship is to disagree but to hold hands.

—Quoted by ALEXANDRA PENNEY in *Self*

The love of our neighbour in all its fullness simply means being able to say to him: "What are you going through?"

—SIMONE WEIL
Waiting for God

The worst prison would be a closed heart.

—POPE JOHN PAUL II

The purest affection the heart can hold is the honest love of a nine-year-old.

—HOLMAN F. DAY
Up in Maine

I love you, not only for what you are, but for what I am when I am with you.

—ROY CROFT

Tell me whom you love, and I'll tell you who you are.

—CREOLE PROVERB

Love at first sight is easy to understand. It's when two people have been looking at each other for years that it becomes a miracle.

—SAM LEVENSON

Love is not measured by how many times you touch each other but by how many times you reach each other.

—CATHY MORANCY

Nobody has ever measured, even the poets, how much a heart can hold.

—ZELDA FITZGERALD

If only one could tell true love from false love as one can tell mushrooms from toadstools.

—KATHERINE MANSFIELD

Four be the things I'd have been better without: love, curiosity, freckles and doubt.

—DOROTHY PARKER

It is often hard to bear the tears that we ourselves have caused.

The Maxims of Marcel Proust

Never close your lips to those to whom you have opened your heart.

—CHARLES DICKENS

To love and be loved is to feel the sun from both sides.

—DAVID VISCOTT, MD
How to Live with Another Person

Love can achieve unexpected majesty in the rocky soil of misfortune.

—TONY SNOW
in Detroit *News*

Love doesn't make the world go round. Love is what makes the ride worthwhile.

—FRANKLIN P. JONES

When one loves somebody, everything is clear—where to go, what to do—it all takes care of itself and one doesn't have to ask anybody about anything.

—MAXIM GORKY
The Zykovs

Love is like a violin. The music may stop now and then, but the strings remain forever.

—JUNE MASTERS BACHER
Diary of a Loving Heart

Love is an act of faith, and whoever is of little faith is also of little love.

—ERICH FROMM

Love endures only when the lovers love many things together and not merely each other.

—WALTER LIPPMANN

When a woman says, "Ah, I could love you if . . ."—fear not, she already loves you.

—WALTER PULITZER

A woman can say more in a sigh than a man can say in a sermon.

—ARNOLD HAULTAIN
Colombo's Canadian Quotations

We love because it's the only true adventure.

—NIKKI GIOVANNI

Seek not every quality in one individual.

—CONFUCIUS

Love is the magician that pulls man out of his own hat.

—BEN HECHT

There is no surprise more magical than the surprise of being loved. It is God's finger on man's shoulder.

—CHARLES MORGAN
The Fountain

To love is to admire with the heart; to admire is to love with the mind.

—THÉOPHILE GAUTIER

What the world really needs is more love and less paperwork.

—PEARL BAILEY

Never look for a worm in the apple of your eye.

—LANGSTON HUGHES

Anything will give up its secrets if you love it enough.

—GEORGE WASHINGTON CARVER

Love talked about can be easily turned aside, but love demonstrated is irresistible.

—W. STANLEY MOONEYHAM
Come Walk the World

The whole worth of a kind deed lies in the love that inspires it.

—THE TALMUD

A baby is born with a need to be loved—and never outgrows it.

—FRANK A. CLARK

A MARRIED COUPLE . . .

A married couple that plays cards together is just a fight that hasn't started yet.

—GEORGE BURNS
Gracie: A Love Story

Marriage resembles a pair of shears, so joined that they cannot be separated; often moving in opposite directions, yet always punishing anyone who comes between them.

—SYDNEY SMITH

It isn't tying himself to one woman that a man dreads when he thinks of marrying; it's separating himself from all the others.

—HELEN ROWLAND
Violets and Vinegar

Marriage should be a duet—when one sings, the other claps.

—JOE MURRAY

The value of marriage is not that adults produce children, but that children produce adults.

—PETER DE VRIES
The Tunnel of Love

Whoever thinks marriage is a 50–50 proposition doesn't know the half of it.

—FRANKLIN P. JONES
in Quote Magazine

A marriage without conflicts is almost as inconceivable as a nation without crises.

—ANDRÉ MAUROIS
The Art of Living

A happy home is one in which each spouse grants the possibility that the other may be right, though neither believes it.

—DON FRASER

More marriages might survive if the partners realised that sometimes the better comes after the worse.

—DOUG LARSON

One advantage of marriage is that, when you fall out of love with him or he falls out of love with you, it keeps you together until you fall in again.

—JUDITH VIORST
in *Redbook*

Marriage is a covered dish.

—SWISS PROVERB

Love, honour and negotiate.

—ALAN LOY MCGINNIS
The Romance Factor

Almost no one is foolish enough to imagine that he automatically deserves great success in any field of activity; yet almost everyone believes that he automatically deserves success in marriage.

—SYDNEY J. HARRIS

Marriage has teeth, and him bite very hot.

—JAMAICAN PROVERB

Getting married is easy. Staying married is more difficult. Staying happily married for a lifetime should rank among the fine arts.

—ROBERTA FLACK

Marriage is like vitamins: we supplement each other's minimum daily requirements.

—KATHY MOHNKE

A wedding anniversary is the celebration of love, trust, partnership, tolerance and tenacity. The order varies for any given year.

—PAUL SWEENEY

A good marriage is like an incredible retirement fund. You put everything you have into it during your productive life, and over the years it turns from silver to gold to platinum.

—WILLARD SCOTT
The Joy of Living

In every marriage more than a week old, there are grounds for divorce. The trick is to find, and continue to find, grounds for marriage.

—ROBERT ANDERSON
Solitaire & Double Solitaire

It takes a loose rein to keep a marriage tight.

—JOHN STEVENSON

If you made a list of reasons why any couple got married, and another list of the reasons for their divorce, you'd have a lot of overlapping.

—MIGNON MCLAUGHLIN

The concept of two people living together for 25 years without a serious dispute suggests a lack of spirit only to be admired in sheep.

—A. P. HERBERT

Story-writers say that love is concerned only with young people, and the excitement and glamour of romance end at the altar. How blind they are. The best romance is inside marriage; the finest love stories come after the wedding, not before.

—IRVING STONE

The great thing about marriage is that it enables one to be alone without feeling loneliness.

—GERALD BRENAN
Thoughts in a Dry Season

A happy marriage is the world's best bargain.

—O. A. BATTISTA

Marrying for love may be a bit risky, but it is so honest that God can't help but smile on it.

—JOSH BILLINGS

The particular charm of marriage is the duologue, the permanent conversation between two people who talk over everything and everyone.

—CYRIL CONNOLLY
The Unquiet Grave

In marriage, being the right person is as important as finding the right person.

—WILBERT DONALD GOUGH

In a successful marriage, there is no such thing as one's way. There is only the way of both, only the bumpy, dusty, difficult, but always mutual path.

—PHYLLIS MCGINLEY
The Province of the Heart

Chains do not hold a marriage together. It is threads, hundreds of tiny threads, which sew people together through the years.

—SIMONE SIGNORET

All that a husband or wife really wants is to be pitied a little, praised a little, appreciated a little.

—OLIVER GOLDSMITH

Marriage should, I think, always be a little hard and new and strange. It should be breaking your shell and going into another world, and a bigger one.

—ANNE MORROW LINDBERGH

A happy marriage is a long conversation that always seems too short.

—ANDRÉ MAUROIS
Mémoires

The difference between courtship and marriage is the difference between the pictures in a seed catalogue and what comes up.

—JAMES WHARTON

The greatest of all arts is the art of living together.

—WILLIAM LYON PHELPS
Marriage

A sound marriage is not based on complete frankness; it is based on a sensible reticence.

—MORRIS L. ERNST

A successful marriage requires falling in love many times, always with the same person.

—MIGNON MCLAUGHLIN
in *The Atlantic*

You don't marry one person; you marry three: the person you think they are, the person they are, and the person they are going to become as the result of being married to you.

—RICHARD NEEDHAM
You and All the Rest

The goal in marriage is not to think alike, but to think together.

—ROBERT C. DODDS

Married life teaches one invaluable lesson: to think of things far enough ahead not to say them.

—JEFFERSON MACHAMER

The marriages we regard as the happiest are those in which each of the partners believes that he or she got the best of it.

—SYDNEY J. HARRIS

Matrimony is the only game of chance the clergy favour.

—EMILY FERGUSON MURPHY

Nobody will ever win the battle of the sexes. There's too much fraternising with the enemy.

—HENRY KISSINGER

THE GREAT GIFT OF FAMILY LIFE . . .

The great gift of family life is to be intimately acquainted with people you might never even introduce yourself to, had life not done it for you.

—KENDALL HAILEY
The Day I Became an Autodidact

Family faces are magic mirrors. Looking at people who belong to us, we see the past, present and future. We make discoveries about ourselves.

—GAIL LUMET BUCKLEY
The Hornes: An American Family

Parentage is a very important profession; but no test of fitness for it is ever imposed in the interests of the children.

—BERNARD SHAW
Everybody's Political What's What?

A happy family is but an earlier heaven.

—JOHN BOWRING

Other things may change us, but we start and end with family.

—ANTHONY BRANDT in *Esquire*

No matter how many communes anybody invents, the family always creeps back.

—MARGARET MEAD

Heredity is what sets the parents of a teenager wondering about each other.

—LAURENCE J. PETER
Peter's Quotations

Heredity is a splendid phenomenon that relieves us of responsibility for our shortcomings.

—DOUG LARSON

Adolescence is perhaps nature's way of preparing parents to welcome the empty nest.

—KAREN SAVAGE AND PATRICIA ADAMS
The Good Stepmother

Few things are more satisfying than seeing your children have teenagers of their own.

—DOUG LARSON

Even a family tree has to have some sap.

—Los Angeles Times Syndicate

Oh, to be only half as wonderful as my child thought I was when he was small, and only half as stupid as my teenager now thinks I am.

—REBECCA RICHARDS

We never know the love of the parent until we become parents ourselves.

—HENRY WARD BEECHER

He that has no fools, knaves nor beggars in his family was begot by a flash of lightning.

—THOMAS FULLER

If you don't believe in ghosts, you've never been to a family reunion.

—ASHLEIGH BRILLIANT

The family fireside is the best of schools.

—ARNOLD H. GLASOW

Before most people start boasting about their family tree, they usually do a good pruning job.

—O. A. BATTISTA

There is no king who has not had a slave among his ancestors, and no slave who has not had a king among his.

—HELEN KELLER

Making the decision to have a child—it's momentous. It is to decide forever to have your heart go walking around outside your body.

—ELIZABETH STONE

When you are a mother, you are never really alone in your thoughts. A mother always has to think twice, once for herself and once for her child.

—SOPHIA LOREN
Women and Beauty

Mothers are the most instinctive philosophers.

—HARRIET BEECHER STOWE

You never get over being a child, long as you have a mother to go to.

—SARAH ORNE JEWETT

A good father is a little bit of a mother.

—LEE SALK

Instant availability without continuous presence is probably the best role a mother can play.

—LOTTE BAILYN
The Woman in America

The three most beautiful sights: a potato garden in bloom, a ship in sail, a woman after the birth of her child.

—IRISH PROVERB

Every parent is at some time the father of the unreturned prodigal, with nothing to do but keep his house open to hope.

—JOHN CIARDI

The most important thing a father can do for his children is to love their mother.

—THEODORE HESBURGH

One father is worth more than a hundred schoolmasters.

—GEORGE HERBERT

My father didn't tell me how to live; he lived, and let me watch him do it.

—CLARENCE BUDINGTON KELLAND

Grandchildren are God's way of compensating us for growing old.

—MARY H. WALDRIP

You don't raise heroes; you raise sons. And if you treat them like sons, they'll turn out to be heroes, even if it's just in your own eyes.

—WALTER SCHIRRA SR.

The beauty of "spacing" children many years apart lies in the fact that parents have time to learn from the mistakes that were made with the older ones—which permits them to make exactly the opposite mistakes with the younger ones.

—SYDNEY J. HARRIS

The thorn from the bush one has planted, nourished and pruned, pricks most deeply and draws more blood.

—MAYA ANGELOU
All God's Children Need Traveling Shoes

It doesn't matter who my father was; it matters who I remember he was.

—ANN SEXTON

Parenthood remains the greatest single preserve of the amateur.

—ALVIN TOFFLER
Future Shock

The word *no* carries a lot more meaning when spoken by a parent who also knows how to say yes.

—JOYCE MAYNARD
in *Parenting*

Lucky parents who have fine children usually have lucky children who have fine parents.

—JAMES A. BREWER

Few things are more delightful than grandchildren fighting over your lap.

—DOUG LARSON

A grandmother is a person with too much wisdom to let that stop her from making a fool of herself over her grandchildren.

—PHIL MOSS
in *National Enquirer*

I have often thought what a melancholy world this would be without children—and what an inhuman world without the aged.

—SAMUEL TAYLOR COLERIDGE

There's nothing like having grandchildren to restore your faith in heredity.

—DOUG LARSON

The simplest toy, one which even the youngest child can operate, is called a grandparent.

—SAM LEVENSON
You Don't Have to Be in "Who's Who" to Know What's What

I don't know who my grandfather was. I am much more concerned to know what his grandson will be.

—ABRAHAM LINCOLN

Nobody can do for little children what grandparents do. Grandparents sort of sprinkle stardust over the lives of little children.

—ALEX HALEY
in *The Maroon*

CHILDREN ARE THE LIVING MESSAGES . . .

Children are the living messages we send to a time we will not see.

—JOHN W. WHITEHEAD
The Stealing of America

Every child comes with the message that God is not yet discouraged of man.

—RABINDRANATH TAGORE

Children are the anchors that hold a mother to life.

—SOPHOCLES

It is not easy to be crafty and winsome at the same time, and few accomplish it after the age of six.

—JOHN W. GARDNER AND
FRANCESCA GARDNER REESE
in *Know or Listen to Those Who Know*

Cherishing children is the mark of a civilised society.

—JOAN GANZ COONEY

Perhaps parents would enjoy their children more if they stopped to realise that the film of childhood can never be run through for a second showing.

—EVELYN NOWN

Human beings are the only creatures on earth that allow their children to come back home.

—BILL COSBY
Fatherhood

Life affords no greater responsibility, no greater privilege, than the raising of the next generation.

—C. EVERETT KOOP, MD

Children have more need of models than of critics.

—CAROLYN COATS
*Things Your Dad Always Told You But
You Didn't Want to Hear*

The greatest natural resource that any country can have is its children.

—DANNY KAYE

Although today there are many trial marriages, there is no such thing as a trial child.

—GARY WILLS

I still live in and on the sunshine of my childhood.

—CHRISTIAN MORGENSTERN

In the little world in which children have their existence, whosoever brings them up, there is nothing so finely perceived and so finely felt as injustice.

—CHARLES DICKENS

Children are innocent and love justice, while most adults are wicked and prefer mercy.

—G. K. CHESTERTON

Children's talent to endure stems from their ignorance of alternatives.

—MAYA ANGELOU

When I was a child, love to me was what the sea is to a fish: something you swim in while you are going about the important affairs of life.

—P. L. TRAVERS

There are no seven wonders of the world in the eyes of a child. There are seven million.

—WALT STREIGHTIFF

The penalty for censoring what your children may be taught is children who are brighter than you.

—FRANK A. CLARK

Ask your child what he wants for dinner only if he's buying.

—FRAN LEBOWITZ
Social Studies

If there is anything we wish to change in the child, we should first examine it and see whether it is not something that could better be changed in ourselves.

—CARL G. JUNG
The Development of Personality

Any child can tell you that the sole purpose of a middle name is so he can tell when he's really in trouble.

—DENNIS FAKES
Points with Punch

When I approach a child, he inspires in me two sentiments: tenderness for what he is, and respect for what he may become.

—LOUIS PASTEUR

We worry about what a child will be tomorrow, yet we forget that he is someone today.

—STACIA TAUSCHER

If children grew up according to early indications, we should have nothing but geniuses.

—JOHANN WOLFGANG VON GOETHE

A child is the root of the heart.

—CAROLINA MARÍA DE JESÚS

There never was a child so lovely but his mother was glad to get him asleep.

—RALPH WALDO EMERSON

Telling a teenager the facts of life
is like giving a fish a bath.
—Arnold H. Glasow

Children have never been good at
listening to their elders, but they
have never failed to imitate them.
—James Baldwin

Oh, what a tangled web do
parents weave when they think
that their children are naïve.
—Ogden Nash

Babies are always more trouble
than you thought—and more
wonderful.
—Charles Osgood
"CBS Morning News"

The one thing children wear out
faster than shoes is parents.
—John J. Plomp

Children aren't happy with
nothing to ignore,
And that's what parents were
created for.
—Ogden Nash

Parents are the bones on which
children cut their teeth.
—Peter Ustinov
in *National Enquirer*

When everything is astonishing,
nothing is astonishing; this is how
the world is to children.
—Antoine Rivaroli

Play is often talked about as if it
were a relief from serious
learning. But for children play is
serious learning. Play is really the
work of childhood.
—Fred Rogers

Having a young child explain
something exciting he has
seen is the finest example of
communication you will ever hear
or see.
—Bob Talbert

There's nothing that can help you
understand your beliefs more than
trying to explain them to an
inquisitive child.
—Frank A. Clark

The greatest aid to adult education
is children.
—Charlie T. Jones and Bob Phillips
Wit & Wisdom

Children are like wet cement.
Whatever falls on them makes an
impression.
—Haim Ginott

Children are not things to be
moulded, but are people
to be unfolded.
—Jess Lair

The best things you can give
children, next to good habits, are
good memories.
—Sydney J. Harris

You don't really understand
human nature unless you know
why a child on a merry-go-round
will wave at his parents every
time around—and why his parents
will always wave back.

—WILLIAM D. TAMMEUS

A child is not a vase to be filled,
but a fire to be lit.

—RABELAIS

Kids are always the only future
the human race has.

—WILLIAM SAROYAN

The most important thing that
parents can teach their children is
how to get along without them.

—FRANK A. CLARK

If you want your children to keep
their feet on the ground, put some
responsibility on their shoulders.

—ABIGAIL VAN BUREN

Loving a child doesn't mean
giving in to all his whims; to love
him is to bring out the best in
him, to teach him to love what is
difficult.

—NADIA BOULANGER

I have found that the best way to
give advice to your children is to
find out what they want, and then
advise them to do it.

—HARRY S TRUMAN

A child, like your stomach,
doesn't need all you can afford to
give it.

—FRANK A. CLARK

The best security blanket a child
can have is parents who respect
each other.

—JAN BLAUSTONE
The Joy of Parenthood

The best inheritance a parent can
give his children is a few minutes
of his time each day.

—O. A. BATTISTA

Any kid who has two parents
who are interested in him
and has a houseful of books isn't
poor.

—SAM LEVENSON

Sometimes the poorest man
leaves his children the richest
inheritance.

—RUTH E. RENKEL
in *National Enquirer*

The greatest gifts you can give
your children are the roots of
responsibility and the wings of
independence.

—DENIS WAITLEY

A truly rich man is one whose
children run into his arms when
his hands are empty.

—*Spotlight* (Boise, Idaho)

If a child lives with approval, he learns to like himself.

—Dorothy Law Nolte

Parents need to fill a child's bucket of self-esteem so high that the rest of the world can't poke enough holes in it to drain it dry.

—Alvin Price

Every adult needs a child to teach; it's the way adults learn.

—Frank A. Clark

Children are likely to live up to what you believe of them.

—Lady Bird Johnson

If you can't hold children in your arms, please hold them in your heart.

—Mother Clara Hale

You cannot train a horse with shouts and expect it to obey a whisper.

—Dagobert D. Runes
Letters to My Son

What's done to children, they will do to society.

—Dr. Karl Menninger

What a father says to his children is not heard by the world; but it will be heard by posterity.

—Jean Paul Richter

Never fear spoiling children by making them too happy. Happiness is the atmosphere in which all good affections grow.

—Thomas Bray

The only thing worth stealing is a kiss from a sleeping child.

—Joe Houldsworth

MANNERS ARE THE HAPPY WAY . . .

Manners are the happy way of doing things.

—Ralph Waldo Emerson

Manners are a sensitive awareness of the feelings of others. If you have that awareness, you have good manners, no matter what fork you use.

—Emily Post

Most arts require long study and application, but the most useful of all, that of pleasing, requires only the desire.

—Lord Chesterfield

Life is not so short but that there is always time for courtesy.

—Ralph Waldo Emerson

Politeness is the art of selecting among one's real thoughts.

—Madame de Staël

To have a respect for ourselves guides our morals; to have a deference for others governs our manners.

—LAURENCE STERNE

Manners are like the zero in arithmetic; they may not be much in themselves, but they are capable of adding a great deal to the value of everything else.

—FREYA STARK
The Journey's Echo

Etiquette is getting sleepy in company and not showing it.

—HYMAN MAXWELL BERSTON

You can get through life with bad manners, but it's easier with good manners.

—LILLIAN GISH

Diplomacy gets you out of what tact would have kept you out of.

—BRIAN BOWLING

The point of tact is not sharp.

—COLLEEN CARNEY

People with tact have less to retract.

—ARNOLD H. GLASOW

Tact consists in knowing how far we may go too far.

—JEAN COCTEAU
A Call to Order

Tact is the knack of making a point without making an enemy.

—HOWARD W. NEWTON

Tact is the art of making guests feel at home when that's really where you wish they were.

—GEORGE E. BERGMAN
in *Good Housekeeping*

Tact is rubbing out another's mistake instead of rubbing it in.

—*Farmer's Almanac*

Tact is the art of recognising when to be big and when not to belittle.

—BILL COPELAND

Tact is the ability to stay in the middle without getting caught there.

—FRANKLIN P. JONES

Tact is the art of convincing people that they know more than you do.

—RAYMOND MORTIMER

Tact is the art of building a fire under people without making their blood boil.

—FRANKLIN P. JONES

The truly free man is he who knows how to decline a dinner invitation without giving an excuse.

—JULES RENARD

Every generation is convinced there has been a deplorable breakdown of manners.

—BYRON DOBELL
in *American Heritage*

To be agreeable in society, you must consent to be taught many things which you already know.

—TALLEYRAND

It takes a lot of thought and effort and downright determination to be agreeable.

—RAY D. EVERSON

Praise is like champagne; it should be served while it is still bubbling.

—*Robins Reader*

Charm is the quality in others that makes us more satisfied with ourselves.

—HENRI FRÉDÉRIC AMIEL

A gentleman is a man who uses a butter knife when dining alone.

—W. F. DETTLE

Nothing prevents us from being natural so much as the desire to appear so.

—FRANÇOIS DE LA ROCHEFOUCAULD

It is a great mistake for men to give up paying compliments, for when they give up saying what is charming, they give up thinking what is charming.

—OSCAR WILDE

Politeness is to human nature what warmth is to wax.

—ARTHUR SCHOPENHAUER

He who says what he likes, hears what he does not like.

—LEONARD LOUIS LEVINSON

The manner in which it is given is worth more than the gift.

—PIERRE CORNEILLE

To receive a present handsomely and in a right spirit, even when you have none to give in return, is to give one in return.

—LEIGH HUNT
Essays by Leigh Hunt

It is much easier to be a hero than a gentleman.

—LUIGI PIRANDELLO

Never claim as a right what you can ask as a favour.

—JOHN CHURTON COLLINS

To err is human; to refrain from laughing, humane.

—LANE OLINGHOUSE

OUR BETTER SIDE

Some people strengthen the society just by being the kind of people they are.

—John W. Gardner

CHARACTER IS WHAT YOU KNOW YOU ARE . . .

Character is what you know you are, not what others think you are.

—Marva Collins and Civia Tamarkin
Marva Collins' Way

Every one of us has in him a continent of undiscovered character. Blessed is he who acts the Columbus to his own soul.

—Quoted in *Words of Life*, edited by Charles L. Wallis

Character is a strange blending of flinty strength and pliable warmth.

—Robert Shaffer

Men are men before they are lawyers, or physicians, or merchants, or manufacturers; and if you make them capable and sensible men, they will make themselves capable and sensible lawyers or physicians.

—John Stuart Mill

Everyone journeys through character as well as through time. The person one becomes depends on the person one has been.

—Dick Francis
A Jockey's Life: The Biography of Lester Piggott

You can measure a man by the opposition it takes to discourage him.

—Robert C. Savage
Life Lessons

We know what a person thinks not when he tells us what he thinks, but by his actions.

—Isaac Bashevis Singer
in *The New York Times Magazine*

Another flaw in the human character is that everybody wants to build and nobody wants to do maintenance.

—Kurt Vonnegut
Hocus Pocus

The severest test of character is not so much the ability to keep a secret as it is, when the secret is finally out, to refrain from disclosing that you knew it all along.

—Sydney J. Harris

Nearly all men can stand adversity, but if you want to test a man's character, give him power.

—Abraham Lincoln

Character may be manifested in the great moments, but it is made in the small ones.

—Phillips Brooks

Show me the man you honour,
and I will know what kind of
man you are.

—THOMAS CARLYLE

People need responsibility. They
resist assuming it, but they cannot
get along without it.

—JOHN STEINBECK
in *Saturday Review*

If anyone thinks he has no
responsibilities, it is because he
has not sought them out.

—MARY LYON

Duty is a very personal thing. It
is what comes from knowing the
need to take action and not just
a need to urge others to do
something.

—MOTHER TERESA OF CALCUTTA

Our concern is not how to
worship in the catacombs, but
rather how to remain human in
the skyscrapers.

—RABBI ABRAHAM JOSHUA HESCHEL
The Insecurity of Freedom

The treacherous, unexplored areas
of the world are not in continents
or the seas; they are in the minds
and hearts of men.

—ALLEN E. CLAXTON

The truth about a man is, first of
all, what it is that he keeps hidden.

—ANDRÉ MALRAUX

Men show their character in
nothing more clearly than by what
they think laughable.

—JOHANN WOLFGANG VON GOETHE

You can discover more about a
person in an hour of play than in
a year of conversation.

—PLATO

There are two insults no human
being will endure: that he has no
sense of humour, and that he has
never known trouble.

—SINCLAIR LEWIS

Sports do not build character.
They reveal it.

—HEYWOOD HALE BROUN

How a man plays the game shows
something of his character; how
he loses shows all of it.

—*Tribune* (Camden County, Georgia)

In our play we reveal what kind
of people we are.

—OVID

Character consists of what you do
on the third and fourth tries.

—JAMES MICHENER
Chesapeake

You can tell more about a person
by what he says about others than
you can by what others say about
him.

—LEO AIKMAN

You can easily judge the character of a man by how he treats those who can do nothing for him.

—JAMES D. MILES

Character is much easier kept than recovered.

—THOMAS PAINE

The way to gain a good reputation is to endeavour to be what you desire to appear.

—SOCRATES

A good reputation is better than fame.

—LOUIS DUDEK
Epigrams

Reputation is character minus what you've been caught doing.

—MICHAEL IAPOCE
A Funny Thing Happened on the Way to the Boardroom

Life is for one generation; a good name is forever.

—JAPANESE PROVERB

To have lost your reputation is to be dead among the living.

—S. H. SIMMONS

Modesty is to merit what shade is to figures in a picture; it gives it strength and makes it stand out.

—JEAN DE LA BRUYÈRE

Modesty is the clothing of talent.

—PIERRE VERON

He who is slowest in making a promise is most faithful in its performance.

—JEAN-JACQUES ROUSSEAU

The only way to make a man trustworthy is to trust him.

—HENRY L. STIMSON
in *Harper's Magazine*

Will-power is being able to eat just one salted peanut.

—PAT ELPHINSTONE

The best discipline, maybe the only discipline that really works, is self-discipline.

—WALTER KIECHEL III
in *Fortune*

You can find on the outside only what you possess on the inside.

—ADOLFO MONTIEL BALLESTEROS
La honda y la flor

In great matters men show themselves as they wish to be seen; in small matters, as they are.

—GAMALIEL BRADFORD

What lies behind us and what lies before us are small matters compared to what lies within us.

—RALPH WALDO EMERSON

Men may be divided almost any way we please, but I have found the most useful distinction to be made between those who devote their lives to conjugating the verb "to be," and those who spend their lives conjugating the verb "to have."

—SYDNEY J. HARRIS

I see God in every human being.

—MOTHER TERESA OF CALCUTTA

One of the best ways to measure people is to watch the way they behave when something free is offered.

—ANN LANDERS

Say not you know a man entirely till you have divided an inheritance with him.

—JOHANN KASPAR LAVATER

Not what I have but what I do is my kingdom.

—THOMAS CARLYLE

The reputation of a thousand years may be determined by the conduct of one hour.

—JAPANESE PROVERB

Fame is the perfume of heroic deeds.

—SOCRATES

Dollars have never been known to produce character, and character will never be produced by money.

—W. K. KELLOGG
I'll Invest My Money in People

One isn't born one's self. One is born with a mass of expectations, a mass of other people's ideas— and you have to work through it all.

—V. S. NAIPAUL

Don't laugh at a youth for his affectations; he is only trying on one face after another to find a face of his own.

—LOGAN PEARSALL SMITH

It has amazed me that the most incongruous traits should exist in the same person and, for all that, yield a plausible harmony.

—W. SOMERSET MAUGHAM

We spend our time searching for security and hate it when we get it.

—JOHN STEINBECK
America and Americans

Without heroes, we are all plain people and don't know how far we can go.

—BERNARD MALAMUD
The Natural

The great man is he who does not lose his child-heart.

—MENCIUS

No great scoundrel is ever uninteresting.

—MURRAY KEMPTON
in *Newsday* (Long Island, New York)

Characters live to be noticed. People with character notice how they live.

—NANCY MOSER

Man is harder than iron, stronger than stone and more fragile than a rose.

—TURKISH PROVERB

He is ill clothed that is bare of virtue.

—BENJAMIN FRANKLIN

All of us are experts at practising virtue at a distance.

—THEODORE M. HESBURGH

To err is human; to blame it on the other guy is even more human.

—BOB GODDARD

There's man all over for you, blaming on his boots the faults of his feet.

—SAMUEL BECKETT
Waiting for Godot

AN OPTIMIST STAYS UP UNTIL MIDNIGHT . . .

An optimist stays up until midnight to see the new year in. A pessimist stays up to make sure the old year leaves.

—BILL VAUGHAN
in Kansas City *Star*

Perpetual optimism is a force multiplier.

—COLIN POWELL

I will say this about being an optimist—even when things don't turn out well, you are certain they will get better.

—FRANK HUGHES

An optimist thinks this is the best of all worlds. A pessimist fears the same may be true.

—DOUG LARSON

Things will probably come out all right, but sometimes it takes strong nerves just to watch.

—HEDLEY DONOVAN

Cynicism is destructive. Hope is the fuel of social change.

—TONY BENN
Quoted by *Observer* magazine

The optimist already sees the scar over the wound; the pessimist still sees the wound underneath the scar.

—Ernst Schroder

The point of living, and of being an optimist, is to be foolish enough to believe the best is yet to come.

—Peter Ustinov

It doesn't hurt to be optimistic. You can always cry later.

—Lucimar Santos de Lima

Cheerfulness, like spring, opens all the blossoms of the inward man.

—Jean Paul Richter

An optimist is the human personification of spring.

—Susan J. Bissonette

I always prefer to believe the best of everybody—it saves so much trouble.

—Rudyard Kipling

A positive attitude may not solve all your problems, but it will annoy enough people to make it worth the effort.

—Herm Albright

Optimism is an intellectual choice.

—Diana Schneider

The average pencil is seven inches long, with just a half-inch eraser— in case you thought optimism was dead.

—Robert Brault

Both optimists and pessimists contribute to our society. The optimist invents the airplane and the pessimist the parachute.

—Gil Stern

A pessimist? That's a person who has been intimately acquainted with an optimist.

—Elbert Hubbard

The nice part about being a pessimist is that you are constantly being either proven right or pleasantly surprised.

—George F. Will
The Leveling Wind

I don't believe in pessimism. If something doesn't come up the way you want, forge ahead. If you think it's going to rain, it will.

—Clint Eastwood

The pessimist complains about the wind; the optimist expects it to change; the realist adjusts the sails.

—William Arthur Ward

An idealist believes the short run doesn't count. A cynic believes the long run doesn't matter. A realist believes that what is done or left undone in the short run determines the long run.

—SYDNEY J. HARRIS

Pessimism never won any battle.

—DWIGHT D. EISENHOWER

MORALITY IS ITS OWN ADVOCATE . . .

Morality is its own advocate; it is never necessary to apologise for it.

—EDITH L. HARRELL

The three hardest tasks in the world are neither physical feats nor intellectual achievements, but moral acts: to return love for hate, to include the excluded, and to say, "I was wrong."

—SYDNEY J. HARRIS
Pieces of Eight

Moral excellence comes about as a result of habit. We become just by doing just acts, temperate by doing temperate acts, brave by doing brave acts.

—ARISTOTLE

It is much easier to repent of sins that we have committed than to repent of those we intend to commit.

—JOSH BILLINGS

The biggest threat to our well-being is the absence of moral clarity and purpose.

—RICK SHUMAN
in *Time*

We laugh at honour and are shocked to find traitors in our midst.

—C. S. LEWIS
The Abolition of Man

It's discouraging to think how many people are shocked by honesty and how few by deceit.

—NOEL COWARD
Blithe Spirit

A good example is like a bell that calls many to church.

—DANISH PROVERB

One man practising sportsmanship is far better than 50 preaching it.

—KNUTE K. ROCKNE
Coaching

The time is always right to do what is right.

—REV. MARTIN LUTHER KING JR.

We don't work hard enough at the basic human qualities. We must remind ourselves what the simplest and most basic words mean—words like honesty and truth. We have too many complicated pieces of apparatus, machinery, computers, and we're trying to outsmart life with their help. All we think about is how to get on best and how to get more for ourselves. We've gone too far in that direction. We've lost our sense of balance.

—LECH WALESA
Quoted in *The Book of Lech Walesa*

Count no day lost in which you waited your turn, took only your share and sought advantage over no one.

—ROBERT BRAULT

The glory of great men should always be measured by the means they have used to acquire it.

—FRANÇOIS DE LA ROCHEFOUCAULD

To have a right to do a thing is not at all the same as to be right in doing it.

—G. K. CHESTERTON

If you're going to do something tonight that you'll be sorry for tomorrow morning, sleep late.

—HENNY YOUNGMAN

Be on guard against excess. Zeal that is too ardent burns more than it reheats.

—ALEC PELLETIER
Le Festin des Morts

What is right is often forgotten by what is convenient.

—BODIE THOENE
Warsaw Requiem

The arm of the moral universe is long, but it bends towards justice.

—REV. MARTIN LUTHER KING JR.

If you don't want anyone to know, don't do it.

—CHINESE PROVERB

No virtue can be great if it is not constant.

—ALFONSO MILAGRO
Los cinco minutos de Dios

Live so that your friends can defend you but never have to.

—ARNOLD H. GLASOW
in *Forbes* magazine

Always put off until tomorrow what you shouldn't do at all.

—MORRIS MANDEL

You can't run a society or cope with its problems if people are not held accountable for what they do.

—JOHN LEO
in *U.S. News & World Report*

Stigmas are the corollaries of
values. If work, independence,
responsibility, respectability are
valued, then their converse must
be devalued, seen as disreputable.
—GERTRUDE HIMMELFARB
The De-moralization of Society

The essence of immorality is the
tendency to make an exception of
myself.
—JANE ADDAMS

He who does not prevent a crime
when he can, encourages it.
—SENECA

A sense of shame is not a bad
moral compass.
—GEN. COLIN POWELL
My American Journey

One of the misfortunes of our
time is that in getting rid of false
shame we have killed off so much
real shame as well.
—LOUIS KRONENBERGER

If moral behaviour were simply
following rules, we could
programme a computer to be
moral.
—SAMUEL P. GINDER
in *Washington Post*

It is unwise to do unto others as
you would that they do unto you.
Their tastes may not be the same.
—BERNARD SHAW

What you dislike for yourself do
not like for me.
—SPANISH PROVERB

Boredom is a vital problem for the
moralist, since at least half the sins
of mankind are caused by the fear
of it.
—BERTRAND RUSSELL

THE PRINCIPAL MARK OF GENIUS . . .

The principal mark of genius is
not perfection but originality, the
opening of new frontiers.
—ARTHUR KOESTLER
The Act of Creation

Originality is unexplored territory.
You get there by carrying a
canoe—you can't take a taxi.
—ALAN ALDA

The only real voyage of discovery
consists not in seeking new
landscapes but in having new
eyes.
—MARCEL PROUST

You don't get harmony when
everybody sings the same note.
—DOUG FLOYD in *Spokesman Review*
(Spokane, Washington)

Since God made us to be
originals, why stoop to be a copy?
—REV. BILLY GRAHAM

While an original is always hard to find, he is easy to recognise.

—JOHN L. MASON
An Enemy Called Average

The courage to imagine the otherwise is our greatest resource, adding colour and suspense to all our life.

—DANIEL J. BOORSTIN

Discoveries are often made by not following instructions, by going off the main road, by trying the untried.

—FRANK TYGER
in *Forbes* magazine

It is by logic that we prove, but by intuition that we discover.

—HENRI POINCARÉ

Don't expect anything original from an echo.

—Quoted in "The 365 Great Quotes-a-Year Calendar"

Truth always originates in a minority of one, and every custom begins as a broken precedent.

—WILL DURANT

Eventually it comes to you: the thing that makes you exceptional, if you are at all, is inevitably that which must also make you lonely.

—LORRAINE HANSBERRY

If you're strong enough, there are no precedents.

—F. SCOTT FITZGERALD
The Crack-Up, edited by Edmund Wilson

The more original a discovery, the more obvious it seems afterwards.

—ARTHUR KOESTLER
The Act of Creation

To go against the dominant thinking of your friends, of most of the people you see every day, is perhaps the most difficult act of heroism you can perform.

—THEODORE H. WHITE

Every society honours its live conformists and its dead troublemakers.

—MIGNON MCLAUGHLIN

Everyone has talent; what is rare is the courage to follow the talent to the dark place where it leads.

—ERICA JONG

To do what others cannot do is talent. To do what talent cannot do is genius.

—WILL HENRY

When there is an original sound in the world, it wakens a hundred echoes.

—JOHN A. SHEDD
Salt from My Attic

The cynic says, "One man can't do anything." I say, "Only one man can do anything." One man interacting creatively with others can move the world.

—John W. Gardner

Everything has been thought of before, but the difficulty is to think of it again.

—Johann Wolfgang von Goethe

Inspiration is never genuine if it is known as inspiration at the time. True inspiration always steals on a person, its importance not being fully recognised for some time.

—Samuel Butler

The work of the individual still remains the spark that moves mankind forward.

—Igor Sikorsky

The most powerful weapon on earth is the human soul on fire.

—Ferdinand Foch

Whatever comes from the heart carries the heat and colour of its birthplace.

—Oliver Wendell Holmes Sr.

We might define an eccentric as a man who is a law unto himself, and a crank as one who, having determined what the law is, insists on laying it down to others.

—Louis Kronenberger

No two men are alike, and both of them are happy for it.

—Morris Mandel
in *The Jewish Press*

Some people march to a different drummer—and some people polka.

—Los Angeles Times Syndicate

THE REAL SECRET OF PATIENCE . . .

The real secret of patience is to find something else to do in the meantime.

—*Dell Pencil Puzzles and Word Games*

I endeavour to be wise when I cannot be merry, easy when I cannot be glad, content with what cannot be mended and patient when there be no redress.

—Elizabeth Montagu

If you are patient in one moment of anger, you will escape a hundred days of sorrow.

—Chinese epigram

He that can have patience can have what he will.

—Benjamin Franklin

The key to everything is patience. You get the chicken by hatching the egg, not by smashing it.

—Arnold H. Glasow

Patience! The windmill never strays in search of the wind.
—ANDY J. SKLIVIS

Nothing valuable can be lost by taking time.
—ABRAHAM LINCOLN

In any contest between power and patience, bet on patience.
—W. B. PRESCOTT

Beware the fury of a patient man.
—JOHN DRYDEN

Patience is bitter, but its fruit is sweet.
—JEAN-JACQUES ROUSSEAU

Patience is the art of hoping.
—VAUVENARGUES

Be patient with everyone, but above all with yourself.
—ST. FRANCIS DE SALES

Patience is the ability to put up with people you'd like to put down.
—ULRIKE RUFFERT

There is a limit at which forbearance ceases to be a virtue.
—EDMUND BURKE

Patience is something you admire in the driver behind you and scorn in the one ahead.
—MAC MCCLEARY

Waiting is worse than knowing. Grief rends the heart cleanly, that it may begin to heal; waiting shreds the spirit.
—MORGAN LLYWELYN
The Wind from Hastings

There's a fine line between fishing and standing on the shore like an idiot.
—STEVEN WRIGHT

Regardless of how much patience we have, we would prefer never to use any of it.
—JAMES T. O'BRIEN

A man without patience is a lamp without oil.
—ANDRÉS SEGOVIA

Impatience can be a virtue, if you practise it on yourself.
—ROD MCKUEN
1985 Book of Days

He who is impatient waits twice.
—MACK MCGINNIS

One of the great disadvantages of hurry is that it takes such a long time.
—G. K. CHESTERTON

We may be willing to tell a story twice but we are never willing to hear it more than once.
—WILLIAM HAZLITT

How can a society that exists on
instant mashed potatoes,
packaged cake mixes, frozen
dinners, and instant cameras teach
patience to its young?

—PAUL SWEENEY

Patience often gets the credit that
belongs to fatigue.

—FRANKLIN P. JONES

THE DIFFERENCE BETWEEN A
HERO AND A COWARD . . .

The difference between a
hero and a coward is one step
sideways.

—GENE HACKMAN

Life shrinks or expands in
proportion to one's courage.

—*The Diary of Anaïs Nin*
edited by Gunther Stuhlmann

Real courage is when you know
you're licked before you begin,
but you begin anyway and see it
through no matter what.

—HARPER LEE
To Kill a Mockingbird

Courage is being scared to
death—and saddling up anyway.

—JOHN WAYNE

It is often easier to fight for
principles than to live up to them.

—ADLAI E. STEVENSON

Courage is the art of being the
only one who knows you're
scared to death.

—EARL WILSON

Facing it—always facing it—that's
the way to get through. Face it!

—JOSEPH CONRAD

Pain nourishes courage. You can't
be brave if you've only had
wonderful things happen to you.

—MARY TYLER MOORE

Success is never final and failure
never total. It's courage that
counts.

—*Success Unlimited*

Courage is the ladder on which all
the other virtues mount.

—CLARE BOOTHE LUCE

It's when you run away that
you're most liable to stumble.

—CASEY ROBINSON

Curiosity will conquer fear even
more than bravery will.

—JAMES STEPHENS

Courage is often lack of
insight, whereas cowardice in
many cases is based on good
information.

—PETER USTINOV

Bravery never goes out of fashion.

—WILLIAM MAKEPEACE THACKERAY

Keep your fears to yourself, but share your courage.

—Robert Louis Stevenson

You can't test courage cautiously.

—Annie Dillard
An American Childhood

Courage is not the towering oak that sees storms come and go; it is the fragile blossom that opens in the snow.

—Alice Mackenzie Swaim

Courage is contagious. When a brave man takes a stand, the spines of others are stiffened.

—Rev. Billy Graham

The way you overcome shyness is to become so wrapped up in something that you forget to be afraid.

—Lady Bird Johnson

A LITTLE KINDNESS . . .

A little kindness from person to person is better than a vast love for all humankind.

—Richard Dehmel

You cannot do a kindness too soon, for you never know how soon it will be too late.

—Ralph Waldo Emerson

The everyday kindness of the back roads more than makes up for the acts of greed in the headlines.

—Charles Kuralt
On the Road With Charles Kuralt

A profusion of pink roses bending ragged in the rain speaks to me of all gentleness and its enduring.

—*The Collected Later Poems
of William Carlos Williams*

Resolve to be tender with the young, compassionate with the aged, sympathetic with the striving, and tolerant with the weak and the wrong. Sometime in life you will have been all of these.

—Bob Goddard

The heart is the toughest part of the body. Tenderness is in the hands.

—Carolyn Forché
The Country Between Us

Life is short and we never have enough time for gladdening the hearts of those who travel the way with us. Oh, be swift to love! Make haste to be kind.

—Henri Frédéric Amiel

There is nothing stronger in the world than gentleness.

—HAN SUYIN
A Many-Splendored Thing

How sweet it is when the strong are also gentle!

—LIBBIE FUDIM

Kindness consists in loving people more than they deserve.

—JOSEPH JOUBERT

Kindness is never wasted. If it has no effect on the recipient, at least it benefits the bestower.

—S. H. SIMMONS

Write injuries in sand, kindnesses in marble.

—FRENCH PROVERB

Ask any decent person what he thinks matters most in human conduct: five to one his answer will be "kindness."

—KENNETH CLARK

Two important things are to have a genuine interest in people and to be kind to them. Kindness, I've discovered, is everything in life.

—ISAAC BASHEVIS SINGER

Always try to be a little kinder than is necessary.

—JAMES M. BARRIE

Kindness is more important than wisdom, and the recognition of this is the beginning of wisdom.

—THEODORE ISAAC RUBIN, MD
One to One

When I was young, I admired clever people. Now that I am old, I admire kind people.

—ABRAHAM JOSHUA HESCHEL

How beautiful a day can be when kindness touches it.

—GEORGE ELLISTON

One kind word can warm three winter months.

—JAPANESE PROVERB

Kind words can be short and easy to speak, but their echoes are truly endless.

—MOTHER TERESA OF CALCUTTA

Tenderness is passion in repose.

—JOSEPH JOUBERT

Kindness is a language which the deaf can hear and the blind can read.

—MARK TWAIN

Kindness can become its own motive. We are made kind by being kind.

—ERIC HOFFER
The Passionate State of Mind

A pat on the back, though only a few vertebrae removed from a kick in the pants, is miles ahead in results.

—Bennett Cerf

A warm smile is the universal language of kindness.

—William Arthur Ward
"Reward Yourself"

When we put ourselves in the other person's place, we're less likely to want to put him in his place.

—Farmer's Digest

Could a greater miracle take place than for us to look through each other's eyes for an instant?

—Henry David Thoreau

You never really understand a person until you consider things from his point of view.

—Harper Lee
To Kill a Mockingbird

Forgive your enemies—if you can't get back at them any other way.

—Franklin P. Jones

Forgiveness is a funny thing. It warms the heart and cools the sting.

—William Arthur Ward

Never does the human soul appear so strong and noble as when it forgoes revenge and dares to forgive an injury.

—E. H. Chapin

One of the most lasting pleasures you can experience is the feeling that comes over you when you genuinely forgive an enemy—whether he knows it or not.

—O. A. Battista
in Quote Magazine

Forgiving and being forgiven are two names for the same thing. The important thing is that a discord has been resolved.

—C. S. Lewis

He who cannot forgive others destroys the bridge over which he himself must pass.

—George Herbert

When a deep injury is done us, we never recover until we forgive.

—Alan Paton

Forgiveness is a gift of high value. Yet its cost is nothing.

—Betty Smith
A Tree Grows in Brooklyn

One of the secrets of a long and fruitful life is to forgive everybody everything every night before you go to bed.

—Ann Landers

Even in the best, most friendly and simple relations of life, praise and commendation are as indispensable as the oil which greases the wheels of a machine to keep them running smoothly.

—LEO TOLSTOY
War and Peace

Feelings are everywhere—be gentle.

—J. MASAI

He best can pity who has felt the woe.

—JOHN GAY

Praise and blame are much the same for a writer. One is better for your vanity but neither gets you much further with your work.

—JEANETTE WINTERSON
quoted in *The Guardian Weekend*

GOODNESS IS THE ONLY INVESTMENT . . .

Goodness is the only investment that never fails.

—HENRY DAVID THOREAU

On the whole, human beings want to be good, but not too good, and not quite all the time.

—GEORGE ORWELL

All that is worth cherishing in this world begins in the heart, not the head.

—Quoted by SUZANNE CHAZIN in
The New York Times

Ten thousand bad traits cannot make a single good one any the less good.

—ROBERT LOUIS STEVENSON

The line separating good and evil passes not through states, nor between political parties either— but right through every human heart.

—ALEKSANDR I. SOLZHENITSYN
The Gulag Archipelago

Some people strengthen society just by being the kind of people they are.

—JOHN W. GARDNER

Those who bring sunshine to the lives of others cannot keep it from themselves.

—JAMES MATTHEW BARRIE

It's not true that nice guys finish last. Nice guys are winners before the game even starts.

—ADDISON WALKER

Sincerity resembles a spice. Too much repels you and too little leaves you wanting.

—BILL COPELAND

If you haven't any charity in your heart, you have the worst kind of heart trouble.

—BOB HOPE

The work of an unknown good man is like a vein of water flowing hidden underground, secretly making the ground greener.

—THOMAS CARLYLE

Generosity always wins favour, particularly when accompanied by modesty.

—JOHANN WOLFGANG VON GOETHE

People want to know how much you care before they care how much you know.

—JAMES F. HIND
in *The Wall Street Journal*

Goodwill is earned by many acts; it can be lost by one.

—DUNCAN STUART

GRATITUDE IS THE MEMORY OF THE HEART

Gratitude is the memory of the heart.

—J. B. MASSIEU

Swift gratitude is the sweetest.

—GREEK PROVERB

The hardest arithmetic to master is that which enables us to count our blessings.

—ERIC HOFFER
Reflections on the Human Condition

Silent gratitude isn't very much use to anyone.

—G. B. STERN
Robert Louis Stevenson

Feeling gratitude and not expressing it is like wrapping a present and not giving it.

—WILLIAM ARTHUR WARD

One must be poor to know the luxury of giving.

—GEORGE ELIOT

To know the value of generosity, it is necessary to have suffered from the cold indifference of others.

—EUGENE CLOUTIER

Sometimes we need to remind ourselves that thankfulness is indeed a virtue.

—WILLIAM J. BENNETT
The Moral Compass

Appreciation is like an insurance policy. It has to be renewed every now and then.

—DAVE MCINTYRE

PERSEVERANCE IS NOT A LONG RACE . . .

Perseverance is not a long race;
it is many short races one after
another.

—WALTER ELLIOTT
The Spiritual Life

Fall seven times, stand up eight.

—JAPANESE PROVERB

Let me tell you the secret that has
led me to my goal. My strength
lies solely in my tenacity.

—LOUIS PASTEUR

Great works are performed, not
by strength, but by perseverance.

—SAMUEL JOHNSON

Vitality shows not only in the
ability to persist but in the ability
to start over.

—F. SCOTT FITZGERALD

Perseverance is the hard work
you do after you get tired of
doing the hard work you already
did.

—NEWT GINGRICH

By perseverance the snail reached
the ark.

—CHARLES HADDON SPURGEON

Lord, give me the determination
and tenacity of a weed.

—MRS. LEON R. WALTERS

In the confrontation between the
stream and the rock, the stream
always wins—not through strength
but by perseverance.

—H. JACKSON BROWN
A Father's Book of Wisdom

What counts is not necessarily
the size of the dog in the
fight—it's the size of the fight in
the dog.

—DWIGHT D. EISENHOWER

A professional is someone who
can do his best work when he
doesn't feel like it.

—ALISTAIR COOKE

The man who removes a
mountain begins by carrying
away small stones.

—CHINESE PROVERB

If you can find a path with no
obstacles, it probably doesn't lead
anywhere.

—FRANK A. CLARK

Go the extra mile. It's never
crowded.

—*Executive Speechwriter Newsletter*

FOR BETTER OR WORSE

He who praises everybody praises nobody.
—SAMUEL JOHNSON

WE ALL KNOW A FOOL . . .

We all know a fool when we see one—but not when we are one.
—ARNOLD H. GLASOW

It is wise to remember that you are one of those who can be fooled some of the time.
—LAURENCE J. PETER
Peter's Almanac

There is a foolish corner in the brain of the wisest man.
—ARISTOTLE

You will do foolish things, but do them with enthusiasm.
—COLETTE

April 1 is the day upon which we are reminded what we are on the other 364.
—MARK TWAIN

Only a fool tests the depth of the water with both feet.
—AFRICAN PROVERB

Anyone can make a mistake. A fool insists on repeating it.
—ROBERTINE MAYNARD

A fool judges people by the presents they give him.
—CHINESE SAYING

Astrology proves one scientific fact, and one only; there's one born every minute.
—PATRICK MOORE

The ultimate result of shielding men from the effects of folly is to fill the world with fools.
—HERBERT SPENCER
Essays

The surprising thing about young fools is how many survive to become old fools.
—DOUG LARSON

Self-delusion is pulling in your stomach when you step on the scales.
—PAUL SWEENEY

Any fool can criticize, condemn and complain—and most do.
—DALE CARNEGIE
How to Win Friends and Influence People

Anybody with money to burn will easily find someone to tend the fire.
—*Pocket Crossword Puzzles*

Follies change their type but foolishness remains.
—ERICH KASTNER

I'm not denyin' that women are foolish: God Almighty made 'em to match the men.

—GEORGE ELIOT

Let us be thankful for the fools. But for them the rest of us could not succeed.

—MARK TWAIN

Everybody has the right to express what he thinks. That, of course, lets the crackpots in. But if you cannot tell a crackpot when you see one, then you ought to be taken in.

—HARRY S TRUMAN

Some people get lost in thought because it's such unfamiliar territory.

—G. BEHN

A bore is a fellow talker who can change the subject to his topic of conversation faster than you can change it back to yours.

—LAURENCE J. PETER
Peter's Quotations

While intelligent people can often simplify the complex, a fool is more likely to complicate the simple.

—GERALD W. GRUMET, MD
in *Readings*

There are 40 kinds of lunacy, but only one kind of common sense.

—AFRICAN PROVERB

A bore is someone who persists in holding his own views after we have enlightened him with ours.

—MALCOLM S. FORBES

Bores bore each other, too, but it never seems to teach them anything.

—DON MARQUIS

Some people can stay longer in an hour than others can in a week.

—WILLIAM DEAN HOWELLS

A healthy male adult bore consumes each year one-and-a-half times his own weight in other people's patience.

—JOHN UPDIKE
Assorted Prose

Everyone is a bore to someone. That is unimportant. The thing to avoid is being a bore to oneself.

—GERALD BRENAN

A fanatic is someone who can't change his mind and won't change the subject.

—WINSTON CHURCHILL

People who insist on telling their dreams are among the terrors of the breakfast table.

—MAX BEERBOHM

Don't approach a goat from the front, a horse from the back or a fool from any side.

—YIDDISH PROVERB

Human reason is like a drunken man on horseback; set it up on one side, and it tumbles over on the other.

—MARTIN LUTHER

LOST BY INDIFFERENCE . . .

More good things in life are lost by indifference than ever were lost by active hostility.

—ROBERT GORDON MENZIES

Apathy is the glove into which evil slips its hand.

—BODIE THOENE

Love me or hate me, but spare me your indifference.

—LIBBIE FUDIM

I have a very strong feeling that the opposite of love is not hate—it's apathy.

—LEO BUSCAGLIA
Love

It is a perplexing and unpleasant truth that when men have something worth fighting for, they do not feel like fighting.

—ERIC HOFFER
The True Believer

There is nothing harder than the softness of indifference.

—JUAN MONTALVO

The tragedy of modern man is not that he knows less and less about the meaning of his own life but that it bothers him less and less.

—VACLAV HAVEL

Crime expands according to our willingness to put up with it.

—BARRY FARBER

GROW ANGRY SLOWLY . . .

Grow angry slowly—there's plenty of time.

—RALPH WALDO EMERSON

Anger is a wind which blows out the lamp of the mind.

—ROBERT G. INGERSOLL

Anger is not only inevitable, it is necessary. Its absence means indifference, the most disastrous of all human failings.

—ARTHUR PONSONBY

Anger is a symptom, a way of cloaking and expressing feelings too awful to experience directly—hurt, bitterness, grief and, most of all, fear.

—JOAN RIVERS
Still Talking

Getting angry can sometimes be like leaping into a wonderfully responsive sports car, gunning the motor, taking off at high speed and then discovering the brakes are out of order.

—MAGGIE SCARF
in *The New York Times Magazine*

Anyone can become angry. That is easy. But to be angry with the right person, to the right degree, at the right time, for the right purpose and in the right way—that is not easy.

—ARISTOTLE

Anger is a bad counsellor.

—FRENCH PROVERB

Resentment is an extremely bitter diet, and eventually poisonous. I have no desire to make my own toxins.

—NEIL KINNOCK

There's a bit of ancient wisdom that appeals to us: it's a saying that a fight starts only with the second blow.

—HUGH ALLEN

I will permit no man to narrow and degrade my soul by making me hate him.

—BOOKER T. WASHINGTON

My life is in the hands of any fool who makes me lose my temper.

—JOSEPH HUNTER

It is only our bad temper that we put down to being tired or worried or hungry; we put our good temper down to ourselves.

—C. S. LEWIS
Mere Christianity

Temper, if ungoverned, governs the whole man.

—ANTHONY SHAFTESBURY

Temper is a quality that at a critical moment brings out the best in steel and the worst in people.

—WILLIAM P. GROHSE

Revenge has no more quenching effect on emotions than salt water has on thirst.

—WALTER WECKLER

Violence is the last refuge of the incompetent.

—ISAAC ASIMOV

A man that studieth revenge keeps his own wounds green.

—FRANCIS BACON

Getting even throws everything out of balance.

—JOE BROWNE
in *Post-Gazette*
(Pittsburgh, Pennsylvania)

If a small thing has the power to make you angry, does that not indicate something about your size?

—SYDNEY J. HARRIS

I imagine one of the reasons people cling to their hates so stubbornly is because they sense, once hate is gone, they will be forced to deal with pain.

—JAMES BALDWIN

To carry a grudge is like being stung to death by one bee.

—WILLIAM H. WALTON

Nothing lowers the level of conversation more than raising the voice.

—STANLEY HOROWITZ

Not the fastest horse can catch a word spoken in anger.

—CHINESE PROVERB

Speak when you are angry and you will make the best speech you will ever regret.

—AMBROSE BIERCE

The best remedy for a short temper is a long walk.

—JACQUELINE SCHIFF
in *National Enquirer*

GOSSIP NEEDN'T BE FALSE . . .

Gossip needn't be false to be evil—there's a lot of truth that shouldn't be passed around.

—FRANK A. CLARK

There is nothing busier than an idle rumour.

—HERBERT V. PROCHNOW
The New Speaker's Treasury
of Wit and Wisdom

In our appetite for gossip, we tend to gobble down everything before us, only to find, too late, that it is our ideals we have consumed, and we have not been enlarged by the feasts but only diminished.

—PICO IYER
in *Time*

Knowledge is power, if you know it about the right person.

—ETHEL WATTS

A gossip is a person who creates the smoke in which other people assume there's fire.

—DAN BENNETT

Gossip is that which no one claims to like—but everybody enjoys.

—JOSEPH CONRAD

Bad news goes about in clogs, good news in stockinged feet.

—WELSH PROVERB

The gossip of the future may not be a backbiting, nosey, tongue-wagging two-face but a super-megabyte, random-access, digital interface.

—RONALD B. ZEH

Some people will believe anything if it is whispered to them.

—PIERRE DE MARIVAUX

Truth is like a chandelier. Everyone in the room can see it, but they all see it from a different angle.

—PETER USTINOV

Men gossip less than women, but mean it.

—MIGNON MCLAUGHLIN

Scandal is the coin of contemporary celebrity. It keeps the public interested.

—RICHARD CORLISS

He who is caught in a lie is not believed when he tells the truth.

—SPANISH PROVERB

Gossip, unlike river water, flows both ways.

—MICHAEL KORDA

Trying to squash a rumour is like trying to unring a bell.

—SHANA ALEXANDER

A rumour without a leg to stand on will get around some other way.

—JOHN TUDOR in *Omni*

Just because a rumour is idle doesn't mean it isn't working.

—MAURICE SEITTER

To speak ill of others is a dishonest way of praising ourselves.

—WILL DURANT

WHEN FLATTERERS MEET . . .

When flatterers meet, the devil goes to dinner.

—ENGLISH PROVERB

Of all music, that which most pleases the ear is applause. But it has no score. It ends and is carried off by the wind. Nothing remains.

—ENRIQUE SOLARI

Flattery is counterfeit money which, but for vanity, would have no circulation.

—FRANÇOIS DE LA ROCHEFOUCAULD

Beware the flatterer: he feeds you with an empty spoon.

—Cosino DeGregrio

A detour is a straight road which turns on the charm.

—Albert Brie
Le Devoir

Flatterers look like friends, as wolves like dogs.

—George Chapman

The punishment for vanity is flattery.

—Wilhelm Raabe

We protest against unjust criticism, but we accept unearned applause.

—José Narosky
Si todos los sueños

I have yet to be bored by someone paying me a compliment.

—Otto van Isch

Flattery is all right—if you don't inhale.

—Adlai E. Stevenson

Praise, if you don't swallow it, can't hurt you.

—Mort Walker

Praise can be your most valuable asset as long as you don't aim it at yourself.

—O. A. Battista

Fish for no compliments; they are generally caught in shallow water.

—D. Smith

Praise is warming and desirable. But it is an earned thing. It has to be deserved, like a hug from a child.

—Phyllis McGinley
in *The Saturday Evening Post*

Sometimes we deny being worthy of praise, hoping to generate an argument we would be pleased to lose.

—Cullen Hightower

He who praises everybody praises nobody.

—Samuel Johnson

FORBIDDEN FRUIT . . .

While forbidden fruit is said to taste sweeter, it usually spoils faster.

—Abigail Van Buren

A compulsion is a highbrow term for a temptation we're not trying too hard to resist.

—Hugh Allen

Most people want to be delivered from temptation but would like it to keep in touch.

—Robert Orben

Those who flee temptation generally leave a forwarding address.

—LANE OLINGHOUSE

Temptation usually comes in through a door that has deliberately been left open.

—ARNOLD H. GLASOW

Temptations, unlike opportunities, will always give you many second chances.

—O. A. BATTISTA

There is no original sin; it has all been done before.

—LOUIS DUDEK

Be cautious. Opportunity does the knocking for temptation too.

—AL BATT

Being virtuous is no feat once temptation ceases.

—DANISH PROVERB

Nothing makes it easier to resist temptation than a proper bringing-up, a sound set of values—and witnesses.

—FRANKLIN P. JONES

In this era of rapid change, one thing remains constant: it's easier to pray for forgiveness than to resist temptation.

—SOL KENDON

About the only time losing is more fun than winning is when you're fighting temptation.

—TOM WILSON

Come good times or bad, there is always a market for things nobody needs.

—KIN HUBBARD

When there's a lot of it around, you never want it very much.

—PEG BRACKEN
The I Hate to Cook Almanack

LAZINESS HAS MANY DISGUISES . . .

Laziness has many disguises. Soon "winter doldrums" will become "spring fever."

—BERN WILLIAMS
in *National Enquirer*

He who is carried on another's back does not appreciate how far off the town is.

—AFRICAN PROVERB

If you get a reputation as an early riser, you can sleep till noon.

—IRISH PROVERB

Cultivate the habit of early rising. It is unwise to keep the head long on a level with the feet.

—HENRY DAVID THOREAU

Laziness may appear attractive,
but work gives satisfaction.
—ANNE FRANK
The Diary of a Young Girl

The safest road to hell is the
gradual one—the gentle slope,
soft underfoot, without sudden
turnings, without milestones,
without signposts.
—C. S. LEWIS
The Screwtape Letters

Laziness is nothing more than
resting before you get tired.
—JULES RENARD

A lot of what passes for
depression these days is nothing
more than a body saying that it
needs work.
—GEOFFREY NORMAN

Beware of the man who won't be
bothered with details.
—WILLIAM FEATHER SR.

It is better to have loafed and lost
than never to have loafed at all.
—JAMES THURBER

I'm lazy. But it's the lazy people
who invented the wheel and the
bicycle because they didn't like
walking or carrying things.
—LECH WALESA

The day will happen whether or
not you get up.
—JOHN CIARDI

About the only thing that comes
to us without effort is old age.
—GLORIA PITZER

I can do only one thing at a time,
but I can avoid doing many things
simultaneously.
—ASHLEIGH BRILLIANT

What a fearful object a
long-neglected duty gets to be!
—CHAUNCEY WRIGHT

A life of ease is a difficult pursuit.
—WILLIAM COWPER

Most of our so-called reasoning
consists in finding arguments
for going on believing as we
already do.
—JAMES HARVEY ROBINSON
The Mind in the Making

No one ever excused his way to
success.
—DAVE DEL DOTTO
*How to Make Nothing
but Money*

Excuses are the nails used to build
a house of failure.
—DON WILDER AND BILL RECHIN

Whoever wants to be a judge
of human nature should study
people's excuses.

> — FRIEDRICH HEBBEL

Don't tell me how hard you work.
Tell me how much you get done.

> —JAMES LING
> in *Newsweek*

To be idle requires a strong sense
of personal identity.

> —ROBERT LOUIS STEVENSON

There are no shortcuts to any
place worth going.

> —BEVERLY SILLS

The older generation thought
nothing of getting up at five
every morning—and the younger
generation doesn't think much of
it either.

> —JOHN J. WELSH

THE FAULTS OF OTHERS . . .

Rare is the person who can weigh
the faults of others without putting
his thumb on the scales.

> —BYRON J. LANGENFIELD

What we all tend to complain about
most in other people are those
things we don't like about ourselves.

> —WILLIAM WHARTON
> *Tidings*

Only God is in a position to look
down on anyone.

> —SARAH BROWN

The unforgiving man assumes
a judgement that not even
the theologians has [sic] given
to God.

> —SYDNEY J. HARRIS

I have never for one instant seen
clearly within myself. How then
would you have me judge the
deeds of others?

> —MAURICE MAETERLINCK

Moral indignation is jealousy with
a halo.

> —H. G. WELLS

Other people's faults are like bees
—if we don't see them, they don't
harm us.

> —LUIS VIGIL
> *Pensamientos y Observaciones*

Make no judgements where you
have no compassion.

> —ANNE MCCAFFREY
> *Dragonquest*

How much easier it is to be
critical than to be correct.

> —BENJAMIN DISRAELI

I don't like a man to be efficient.
He's likely to be not human enough.

> —FELIX FRANKFRUTER

When a man points a finger at someone else, he should remember that three of his fingers are pointing at himself.
—ANONYMOUS

Ought is not a word we use to other people. It is a word we should reserve for ourselves.
—SISTER WENDY BECKETT

Perhaps no phenomenon contains so much destructive feeling as "moral indignation," which permits envy or hate to be acted out under the guise of virtue.
—ERICH FROMM

If you judge people, you have no time to love them.
—MOTHER TERESA OF CALCUTTA

Speak not against anyone whose burden you have not weighed yourself.
—MARION BRADLEY
Black Trillium

Puritanism is the haunting fear that someone, somewhere, may be happy.
—H. L. MENCKEN

This is a do-it-yourself test for paranoia: you know you've got it when you can't think of anything that's your fault.
—ROBERT M. HUTCHINS

That which we call sin in others is experiment for us.
—RALPH WALDO EMERSON

We all have weaknesses. But I have figured that others have put up with mine so tolerantly that I would be less than fair not to make a reasonable discount for theirs.
—WILLIAM ALLEN WHITE

We are all inclined to judge ourselves by our ideals; others, by their acts.
—HAROLD NICOLSON

Distrust all in whom the impulse to punish is powerful.
—FRIEDRICH NIETZSCHE

Nothing so needs reforming as other people's habits.
—MARK TWAIN

Our faults irritate us most when we see them in others.
—PENNSYLVANIA DUTCH PROVERB

The enthusiastic, to those who are not, are always something of a trial.
—ALBAN GOODIER

There is little room left for wisdom when one is full of judgement.
—MALCOLM HEIN

Nothing in the world is so rare as a person one can always put up with.

—Giacomo Leopardi

When nobody around you seems to measure up, it's time to check your yardstick.

—Bill Lemley

It has been my experience that folks who have no vices have very few virtues.

—Abraham Lincoln

There are certain small faults that offset great virtues. There are certain great faults that are forgotten in small virtues.

—Grantland Rice Watts

Accept me as I am—only then will we discover each other.

—From Federico Fellini's 8 1/2

The less secure a man is, the more likely he is to have extreme prejudices.

—Clint Eastwood

Nothing dies so hard, or rallies so often, as intolerance.

—Henry Ward Beecher

Prejudices are the chains forged by ignorance to keep men apart.

—Countess of Blessington

Prejudice is a disease characterised by hardening of the categories.

—William Arthur

A prejudice is a vagrant opinion without visible means of support.

—Ambrose Bierce

It is never too late to give up our prejudices.

—Henry David Thoreau

Every bigot was once a child free of prejudice.

—Sister Mary De Lourdes

Too many of our prejudices are like pyramids upside down. They rest on tiny, trivial incidents, but they spread upward and outward until they fill our minds.

—William McChesney Martin

STUPIDITY WON'T KILL YOU . . .

Stupidity won't kill you, but it can make you sweat.

—English proverb

Ignorance is not bliss—it is oblivion.

—Philip Wylie

I am patient with stupidity but not with those who are proud of it.

—Edith Sitwell

To be clever enough to get a good deal of money, one must be stupid enough to want it.

—G. K. CHESTERTON

The greatest obstacle to discovering the shape of the earth, the continents and the ocean was not ignorance but the illusion of knowledge.

—DANIEL J. BOORSTIN
The Discoverers

Ignorance is bold, and knowledge reserved.

—THUCYDIDES

Sometimes the best way to convince someone he is wrong is to let him have his way.

—RED O'DONNELL

Preconceived notions are the locks on the door to wisdom.

—MERRY BROWNE
in *National Enquirer*

Fears are educated into us and can, if we wish, be educated out.

—KARL A. MENNINGER, MD
The Human Mind

The intelligent man who is proud of his intelligence is like the condemned man who is proud of his large cell.

—SIMONE WEIL

Everybody is ignorant, only on different subjects.

—WILL ROGERS

IF MALICE OR ENVY WERE TANGIBLE . . .

It is never wise to seek or wish for another's misfortune. If malice or envy were tangible and had a shape, it would be the shape of a boomerang.

—CHARLEY REESE

Spite is never lonely; envy always tags along.

—MIGNON MCLAUGHLIN

Envy is the art of counting the other fellow's blessings instead of your own.

—HAROLD COFFIN

Do not believe those persons who say they have never been jealous. What they mean is that they have never been in love.

—GERALD BRENAN

Love looks through a telescope; envy, through a microscope.

—JOSH BILLINGS

Jealousy is all the fun you think they had.

—ERICA JONG

I'd never try to learn from someone I didn't envy at least a little. If I never envied, I'd never learn.

—BETSY COHEN
The Snow White Syndrome

THE CHAINS OF HABIT . . .

The chains of habit are generally too small to be felt until they are too strong to be broken.

—SAMUEL JOHNSON

Good habits are as easy to form as bad ones.

—TIM MCCARVER

Habits are first cobwebs, then cables.

—SPANISH PROVERB

Comfort comes as a guest, lingers to become a host and stays to enslave us.

—LEE S. BICKMORE

Habit is habit, and not to be flung out of the window by any man, but coaxed downstairs a step at a time.

—MARK TWAIN

A habit is something you can do without thinking—which is why most of us have so many of them.

—FRANK A. CLARK

The best way to break a habit is to drop it.

—LEO AIKMAN

Habits are like supervisors that you don't notice.

—HANNES MESSEMER

We can often endure an extra pound of pain far more easily than we can suffer the withdrawal of an ounce of accustomed pleasure.

—SYDNEY J. HARRIS

Habit, if not resisted, soon becomes necessity.

—ST. AUGUSTINE

It is easy to assume a habit; but when you try to cast it off, it will take skin and all.

—JOSH BILLINGS

A habit is a shirt made of iron.

—HAROLD HELFER

A bad habit never disappears miraculously; it's an undo-it-yourself project.

—ABIGAIL VAN BUREN

NEVER BE HAUGHTY . . .

Never be haughty to the humble. Never be humble to the haughty.

—JEFFERSON DAVIS

None are so empty as those who are full of themselves.

—Benjamin Whichcote

The louder he talked of his honour, the faster we counted our spoons.

—Ralph Waldo Emerson

He who truly knows has no occasion to shout.

—Leonardo da Vinci

The question we do not see when we are young is whether we own pride or are owned by it.

—Josephine Johnson
The Dark Traveler

If you are all wrapped up in yourself, you are overdressed.

—*The Wedded Unmother*

A man wrapped up in himself makes a very small parcel.

—"Thought for the Day," BBC Radio

When someone sings his own praises, he always gets the tune too high.

—Mary H. Waldrip

Lord, where we are wrong, make us willing to change; where we are right, make us easy to live with.

—Rev. Peter Marshall

Vanity is the result of a delusion that someone is paying attention.

—Paul E. Sweeney

Too great a sense of identity makes a man feel he can do no wrong. And too little does the same.

—Djuna Barnes

Oh, for a pin that would puncture pretension!

—Isaac Asimov
Buy Jupiter and Other Stories

It is far more impressive when others discover your good qualities without your help.

—Judith S. Martin

A modest man is usually admired— if people ever hear of him.

—Ed Howe

The nice thing about egotists is that they don't talk about other people.

—Lucille S. Harper

The egotist always hurts the one he loves—himself.

—Bernice Peers

The only cure for vanity is laughter. And the only fault that's laughable is vanity.

—Henri Bergson

WHEN WE ACT

Life is a great big canvas, and you should throw all the paint on it you can.

—Danny Kaye

THE VERY ESSENCE OF LEADERSHIP . . .

The very essence of leadership is that you have to have a vision. You can't blow an uncertain trumpet.

—THEODORE HESBURGH

High sentiments always win in the end. The leaders who offer blood, toil, tears and sweat always get more out of their followers than those who offer safety and a good time. When it comes to the pinch, human beings are heroic.

—GEORGE ORWELL
Collected Essays, Journalism and Letters

Consensus is the negation of leadership.

—MARGARET THATCHER

You do not lead by hitting people over the head. That's assault, not leadership.

—DWIGHT D. EISENHOWER

Never tell people how to do things. Tell them what to do and they will surprise you with their ingenuity.

—GEN. GEORGE S. PATTON JR.

Anyone can hold the helm when the sea is calm.

—PUBLILIUS SYRUS

Rules are made for people who aren't willing to make up their own.

—CHUCK YEAGER AND
CHARLES LEERHSEN
Press On!

A leader knows what's best to do; a manager knows merely how best to do it.

—KEN ADELMAN

Leadership is a potent combination of strategy and character. But if you must be without one, be without the strategy.

—GEN. H. NORMAN SCHWARZKOPF

A leader who keeps his ear to the ground allows his rear end to become a target.

—ANGIE PAPADAKIS

The person who knows how will always have a job. But the person who knows why will be his boss.

—CARL C. WOOD

It's easy to make a buck. It's a lot tougher to make a difference.

—TOM BROKAW

One measure of leadership is the calibre of people who choose to follow you.

—DENNIS A. PEER

Nothing great was ever achieved without enthusiasm.

—RALPH WALDO EMERSON

Knowledge cannot make us all leaders, but it can help us decide which leader to follow.

—*Management Digest*

Wise are those who learn that the bottom line doesn't always have to be their top priority.

—WILLIAM ARTHUR WARD

The mark of a true professional is giving more than you get.

—ROBERT KIRBY

We still think of a powerful man as a born leader and a powerful woman as an anomaly.

—MARGARET ATWOOD

A man who enjoys responsibility usually gets it. A man who merely likes exercising authority usually loses it.

—MALCOLM S. FORBES

Few things are harder to put up with than the annoyance of a good example.

—MARK TWAIN

He that would be a leader must be a bridge.

—WELSH PROVERB

A leader does not impose a decision, he moulds one.

—NELSON MANDELA

The speed of the leader determines the rate of the pack.

—WAYNE LUKAS

If you want truly to understand something, try to change it.

—KURT LEWIN

Rank does not confer privilege or give power. It imposes responsibility.

—PETER DRUCKER
in *Fortune*

Asking "Who ought to be boss?" is like asking "Who ought to be the tenor in the quartet?" Obviously, the man who can sing tenor.

—HENRY FORD

A great leader is the one who can show people that their self-interest is different from that which they perceived.

—BARNEY FRANK

No person can be a great leader unless he takes genuine joy in the successes of those under him.

—W. A. NANCE

First-rate men hire first-rate men;
second-rate men hire third-rate
men.

—LEO ROSTEN

The things we fear most in
organisations—fluctuations,
disturbances, imbalances—are the
primary sources of creativity.

—MARGARET J. WHEATLEY
Leadership and the New Science

Change starts when someone sees
the next step.

—WILLIAM DRAYTON
in *Esquire*

I am more afraid of an army of
100 sheep led by a lion than an
army of 100 lions led by a sheep.

—TALLEYRAND

It's better to be a lion for a day
than a sheep all your life.

—SISTER KENNY

WHAT GREAT THING WOULD
YOU ATTEMPT . . .

What great thing would you
attempt if you knew you could
not fail?

—ROBERT H. SCHULLER

Why not upset the apple cart?
If you don't, the apples will rot
anyway.

—FRANK A. CLARK

When a man's willing and eager,
the gods join in.

—AESCHYLUS

Determine that the thing can and
shall be done, and then we shall
find the way.

—ABRAHAM LINCOLN

Trust in God and do something.

—MARY LYON

Action may not always be
happiness, but there is no
happiness without action.

—BENJAMIN DISRAELI

In the West there is a widespread
view that the Russian people
cannot build their own future. We
will never get anything until we
realise that we are masters of our
own fate.

—ALEKSANDR SOLZHENITSYN

Noble deeds and hot baths are the
best cures for depression.

—DODIE SMITH
I Capture the Castle

My view is that to sit back and let
fate play its hand out and never
influence it is not the way man
was meant to operate.

—JOHN GLENN

All glory comes from daring to
begin.

—EUGENE F. WARE

People judge you by your actions, not your intentions. You may have a heart of gold, but so has a hard-boiled egg.

—*Good Reading*

Let him that would move the world, first move himself.

—Socrates

Everything comes to he who hustles while he waits.

—Thomas A. Edison

Well done is better than well said.

—Benjamin Franklin

You can't build a reputation on what you are going to do.

—Henry Ford

If you never budge, don't expect a push.

—Malcolm S. Forbes

It is easy to sit up and take notice. What is difficult is getting up and taking action.

—Al Batt

Dig the well before you are thirsty.

—Chinese proverb

Life is a great big canvas, and you should throw all the paint on it you can.

—Danny Kaye

Pennies do not come from heaven. They have to be earned here on earth.

—Margaret Thatcher

Success is a ladder that cannot be climbed with your hands in your pockets.

—American proverb

Have you considered that if you "don't make waves," nobody, including yourself, will know that you are alive?

—Theodore Isaac Rubin, MD

Many a man with no family tree has succeeded because he branched out for himself.

—Leo Aikman

God gives every bird his worm, but he does not throw it into the nest.

—Swedish proverb

Ask God's blessing on your work, but don't ask him to do it for you.

—Dame Flora Robson
on *Friends*, BBC

You must get involved to have an impact. No one is impressed with the won-lost record of the referee.

—John H. Holcomb
The Militant Moderate

Not everything that is faced can be changed. But nothing can be changed until it is faced.

—JAMES BALDWIN

Our dilemma is that we hate change and love it at the same time; what we really want is for things to remain the same but get better.

—SYDNEY J. HARRIS

Just as iron rusts from disuse, even so does inaction spoil the intellect.

—LEONARDO DA VINCI

Men may doubt what you say, but they will believe what you do.

—LEWIS CASS

If your ship doesn't come in, swim out to it!

—JONATHAN WINTERS

Sow an act, and you reap a habit. Sow a habit, and you reap a character. Sow a character, and you reap a destiny.

—CHARLES READE

BE BOLD IN WHAT YOU STAND FOR . . .

Be bold in what you stand for and careful what you fall for.

—RUTH BOORSTIN
in *The Wall Street Journal*

Don't believe that winning is really everything. It's more important to stand for something. If you don't stand for something, what do you win?

—LANE KIRKLAND

Never give in—in nothing, great or small, large or petty—except to convictions of honour and good sense.

—WINSTON CHURCHILL

The quality of a man's life is in direct proportion to his commitment to excellence, regardless of his chosen field of endeavour.

—VINCE LOMBARDI

A good resolution is like an old horse which is often saddled but rarely ridden.

—MEXICAN PROVERB

Compromise makes a good umbrella, but a poor roof.

—JAMES RUSSELL LOWELL

A thing moderately good is not so good as it ought to be. Moderation in temper is always a virtue; but moderation in principle is always a vice.

—THOMAS PAINE

Middleness is the very enemy of the bold.

—CHARLES KRAUTHAMMER

He that always gives way to others will end in having no principles of his own.

—AESOP

You've got to stand for somethin' or you're gonna fall for anything.

—JOHN COUGAR MELLENCAMP
"You've Got to Stand
for Somethin'"

Learn to say no. It will be of more use to you than to be able to read Latin.

—CHARLES HADDON SPURGEON

Half the troubles of this life can be traced to saying yes too quickly and not saying no soon enough.

—JOSH BILLINGS

It's important that people should know what you stand for. It's equally important that they know what you won't stand for.

—MARY H. WALDRIP

A man's judgement is best when he can forget himself and any reputation he may have acquired and can concentrate wholly on making the right decisions.

—ADM. RAYMOND A. SPRUANCE

Standing in the middle of the road is very dangerous; you get knocked down by the traffic from both sides.

—MARGARET THATCHER

The most prominent place in hell is reserved for those who are neutral on the great issues of life.

—REV. BILLY GRAHAM

Never "for the sake of peace and quiet" deny your own experience or convictions.

—DAG HAMMARSKJÖLD

When something important is going on, silence is a lie.

—A. M. ROSENTHAL
in The New York Times

Please all and you please none.

—AESOP

He who turns the other cheek too far gets it in the neck.

—H. HERT

You can lean over backward so far that you fall flat on your face.

—BEN H. BAGDIKIAN

In the end it will not matter to us whether we fought with flails or reeds. It will matter to us greatly on what side we fought.

—G. K. CHESTERTON

OPPORTUNITIES ARE NEVER LOST . . .

Opportunities are never lost. The other fellow takes those you miss.

—ANONYMOUS

Not many sounds in life, and I include all urban and all rural sounds, exceed in interest a knock at the door.

—CHARLES LAMB

The world is before you, and you need not take it or leave it as it was when you came in.

—JAMES BALDWIN

Opportunity is often difficult to recognise; we usually expect it to beckon us with beepers and billboards.

—WILLIAM ARTHUR WARD

If opportunity doesn't knock, build a door.

—MILTON BERLE

It is often hard to distinguish between the hard knocks in life and those of opportunity.

—FREDERICK PHILLIPS

Life is always walking up to us and saying, "Come on in, the living's fine," and what do we do? Back off and take its picture.

—RUSSELL BAKER

Opportunity is sometimes hard to recognise if you're only looking for a lucky break.

—MONTA CRANE

Opportunity's favourite disguise is trouble.

—FRANK TYGER
in *Rotary "Scandal Sheet"*
(Graham, Texas)

Opportunities are often things you haven't noticed the first time around.

—CATHERINE DENEUVE

Wherever we look upon this earth, the opportunities take shape within the problems.

—NELSON A. ROCKEFELLER

If a window of opportunity appears, don't pull down the shade.

—TOM PETERS
The Pursuit of Wow!

Jumping at several small opportunities may get us there more quickly than waiting for one big one to come along.

—HUGH ALLEN

Curiosity opens the doors and you choose which ones to go through.

—BARONESS DENTON
in *Telegraph Magazine*

A problem is a chance for you to do your best.

—DUKE ELLINGTON

If you can see a bandwagon, it's too late to get on it.

—SIR JAMES GOLDSMITH
quoted in *Tycoon*

Problems are only opportunities with thorns on them.

—HUGH MILLER
Snow on the Wind

Opportunity is a bird that never perches.

—CLAUDE McDONALD

One of the secrets of life is to make stepping stones out of stumbling blocks.

—JACK PENN

Today's opportunities erase yesterday's failures.

—GENE BROWN
in *News-Times* (Danbury, Connecticut)

I make the most of all that comes and the least of all that goes.

—SARA TEASDALE
"The Philosopher," in *Poems That Touch the Heart*, edited by A. L. Alexander

Everyone's eyes ought to be windows, but in too many cases they are shutters instead.

—PAUL BAILEY
in *The Daily Telegraph*

OUT ON A LIMB . . .

Why not go out on a limb? Isn't that where the fruit is?

—FRANK SCULLY

All growth, including political growth, is the result of risk-taking.

—JUDE WANNISKI

What isn't tried won't work.

—CLAUDE McDONALD
in *The Christian Word*

What is more mortifying than to feel that you have missed the plum for want of courage to shake the tree?

—LOGAN PEARSALL SMITH

It is not because things are difficult that we do not dare; it is because we do not dare that they are difficult.

—SENECA

What would life be if we had no courage to attempt anything?

—VINCENT VAN GOGH

A coward meets his fate in his own hideout.

—JORGE SALVADOR LARA
El Comercio

All serious daring starts from within.

—EUDORA WELTY
One Writer's Beginnings

If you risk nothing, then you risk everything.

—GEENA DAVIS

Worry is like a rocking chair. It will give you something to do, but it won't get you anywhere.

—*The United Church Observer*

Take a chance! All life is a chance. The man who goes furthest is generally the one who is willing to do and dare.

—*Dale Carnegie's Scrapbook*, edited by Dorothy Carnegie

People wish to learn to swim and at the same time to keep one foot on the ground.

—MARCEL PROUST
Remembrance of Things Past

High expectations are the key to everything.

—SAM WALTON

If you're never scared or embarrassed or hurt, it means you never take any chances.

—JULIA SOREL

When you're skating on thin ice, you may as well tap-dance.

—BRYCE COURTENAY

It's better to plunge into the unknown than to try to make sure of everything.

—GERALD LESCARBEAULT

Take calculated risks. That is quite different from being rash.

—GEN. GEORGE S. PATTON JR.

We cannot become what we need to be by remaining what we are.

—MAX DE PREE
Leadership Is an Art

When you reach for the stars, you may not quite get one, but you won't come up with a handful of mud either.

—LEO BURNETT

In skating over thin ice, our safety is in our speed.

—RALPH WALDO EMERSON

You are permitted in time of great danger to walk with the devil until you have crossed the bridge.

—BULGARIAN PROVERB

If you don't place your foot on the rope, you'll never cross the chasm.

—LIZ SMITH

Necessity is the mother of taking chances.

—MARK TWAIN

If necessity is the mother of invention, discontent is the father of progress.

—DAVID ROCKEFELLER

Sometimes the fool who rushes in gets the job done.

—AL BERNSTEIN

A ship in harbour is safe—but that is not what ships are for.

—JOHN A. SHEDD

Don't be afraid of failure, it's a stepping-stone to success.

—OPRAH WINFREY

A ROAD TWICE TRAVELLED . . .

A road twice travelled is never as long.

—ROSALIE GRAHAM

The meaning of life cannot be told; it has to happen to a person.

—IRA PROGOFF
The Symbolic & the Real

The winds and waves are always on the side of the ablest navigators.

—EDWARD GIBBON

The person who has had a bull by the tail once has learned 60 or 70 times as much as a person who hasn't.

—MARK TWAIN

The work will teach you how to do it.

—ESTONIAN PROVERB

Sometimes you earn more doing the jobs that pay nothing.

—TODD RUTHMAN

When you fall in a river, you're no longer a fisherman; you're a swimmer.

—GENE HILL
in *Field & Stream*

Believe one who has tried it.

—VIRGIL

Anybody who profits from the experience of others probably writes biographies.

—FRANKLIN P. JONES

Only the wearer knows where the shoe pinches.

—PROVERB

A man begins cutting his wisdom teeth the first time he bites off more than he can chew.

—HERB CAEN

The value of experience is not in seeing much, but in seeing wisely.

—SIR WILLIAM OSLER

People learn something every day, and a lot of times it's that what they learned the day before was wrong.

—BILL VAUGHAN

We learn to walk by stumbling.

—BULGARIAN PROVERB

One thing about experience is that when you don't have very much you're apt to get a lot.

—FRANKLIN P. JONES
in *Quote*

Experience is a wonderful thing; it enables you to recognise a mistake every time you repeat it.

—The Associated Press

I have never let my schooling interfere with my education.

—MARK TWAIN

Experience is what you get when you don't get what you want.

—DAN STANFORD

Information's pretty thin stuff unless mixed with experience.

—CLARENCE DAY
The Crow's Nest

If we could sell our experiences for what they cost us, we'd all be millionaires.

—ABIGAIL VAN BUREN

Half, maybe more, of the delight of experiencing is to know what you are experiencing.

—JESSAMYN WEST
Hide and Seek

Perhaps the angels who fear to tread where fools rush in used to be fools who rushed in.

—FRANKLIN P. JONES

HE WHO HESITATES . . .

He who hesitates is last.

—*The Wit and Wisdom of Mae West*
edited by Joseph Weintraub

He who hesitates is sometimes saved.

—JAMES THURBER
Fables for Our Time

These things are good in little measure and evil in large: yeast, salt and hesitation.

—*THE TALMUD*

The man who insists upon seeing with perfect clearness before he decides, never decides.

—HENRI FRÉDÉRIC AMIEL

A man would do nothing if he waited until he could do it so well that no one could find fault.

—JOHN HENRY CARDINAL NEWMAN

It's better to be boldly decisive and risk being wrong than to agonise at length and be right too late.

—MARILYN MOATS KENNEDY
Across the Board

If all difficulties were known at the outset of a long journey, most of us would never start out at all.

—DAN RATHER WITH
PETER WYDEN
I Remember

Decision is a sharp knife that cuts clean and straight. Indecision is a dull one that hacks and tears and leaves ragged edges behind.

—Jan McKeithen

The chief danger in life is that you may take too many precautions.

—Alfred Adler

You have to be careful about being too careful.

—Beryl Pfizer

If you wait, all that happens is that you get older.

—Larry McMurtry
Some Can Whistle

If you take too long in deciding what to do with your life, you'll find you've done it.

—Pam Shaw

To think too long about doing a thing often becomes its undoing.

—Eva Young

When you have to make a choice and don't make it, that is in itself a choice.

—William James

Half the failures in life arise from pulling in one's horse as he is leaping.

—Julius Charles Hare
and Augustus William Hare

Give me the benefit of your convictions, if you have any; but keep your doubts to yourself, for I have enough of my own.

—Johann Wolfgang von Goethe

Throughout history, the most common debilitating human ailment has been cold feet.

—*Country*

Retreat as a tactic is sometimes necessary. Retreat as a settled policy eats at the soul.

—Lady Thatcher
The Downing Street Years

Calculation never made a hero.

—John Henry Cardinal Newman

He who hesitates is interrupted.

—Franklin P. Jones

IF YOU CAN'T MAKE A MISTAKE . . .

If you can't make a mistake, you can't make anything.

—Marva N. Collins

The greatest mistake you can make in life is continually to be fearing you will make one.

—Elbert Hubbard

A stumble may prevent a fall.

—English proverb

He who never made a mistake never made a discovery.
—SAMUEL SMILES

A mistake proves that someone stopped talking long enough to do something.
—PHOENIX FLAME

Mistakes are the usual bridge between inexperience and wisdom.
—PHYLLIS THEROUX
Night Lights

Better to ask twice than to lose your way once.
—DANISH PROVERB

We're all proud of making little mistakes. It gives us the feeling we don't make any big ones.
—ANDREW A. ROONEY
Not That You Asked . . .

To err is human; to admit it, superhuman.
—DOUG LARSON

Admit your errors before someone else exaggerates them.
—ANDREW V. MASON, MD

Never let the fear of striking out get in your way.
—BABE RUTH

There is no saint without a past— no sinner without a future.
—ANCIENT PERSIAN MASS

Once we realise that imperfect understanding is the human condition, there is no shame in being wrong, only in failing to correct our mistakes.
—GEORGE SOROS
Soros on Soros

One of the most dangerous forms of human error is forgetting what one is trying to achieve.
—PAUL NITZE

It is very easy to forgive others their mistakes; it takes more grit and gumption to forgive them for having witnessed your own.
—JESSAMYN WEST

The worst part is not in making a mistake but in trying to justify it, instead of using it as a heaven-sent warning of our mindlessness or our ignorance.
—SANTIAGO RAMÓN Y CAJAL
Charlas de Café

Always acknowledge a fault frankly. This will throw those in authority off their guard and give you opportunity to commit more.
—MARK TWAIN

To obtain maximum attention, it's hard to beat a good, big mistake.
—DAVID D. HEWITT

Justifying a fault doubles it.
—FRENCH PROVERB

Your worst humiliation is only someone else's momentary entertainment.

—KAREN CROCKETT

He who is afraid to ask is ashamed of learning.

—DANISH PROVERB

The only nice thing about being imperfect is the joy it brings to others.

—DOUG LARSON

Nine times out of ten, the first thing a man's companion knows of his shortcomings is from his apology.

—OLIVER WENDELL HOLMES SR.

If all else fails, immortality can always be assured by spectacular error.

—JOHN KENNETH GALBRAITH
Money: Whence It Came, Where It Went

I'D RATHER BE A FAILURE . . .

I'd rather be a failure at something I enjoy than be a success at something I hate.

—GEORGE BURNS

Don't confuse fame with success. Madonna is one; Helen Keller is the other.

—ERMA BOMBECK

Victory is in the quality of competition, not the final score.

—MIKE MARSHALL

You never conquer a mountain. You stand on the summit a few moments; then the wind blows your footprints away.

—ARLENE BLUM

Laurels don't make much of a cushion.

—DOROTHY RABINOWITZ

Success covers a multitude of blunders.

—BERNARD SHAW

Failure is the condiment that gives success its flavour.

—TRUMAN CAPOTE

Success and failure. We think of them as opposites, but they're really not. They're companions— the hero and the sidekick.

—LAURENCE SHAMES

The hero reveals the possibilities of human nature; the celebrity reveals the possibilities of the media.

—DANIEL J. BOORSTIN
The Image

Oh, the difference between nearly right and exactly right.

—HORACE J. BROWN

Success is never final, but failure can be.

—BILL PARCELLS
Finding a Way to Win

I couldn't wait for success . . . so I went ahead without it.

—JONATHAN WINTERS

There is no comparison between that which is lost by not succeeding and that which is lost by not trying.

—FRANCIS BACON

You may be disappointed if you fail, but you are doomed if you don't try.

—BEVERLY SILLS

Use what talents you possess: the woods would be very silent if no birds sang there except those that sang best.

—HENRY VAN DYKE

Ability is what you're capable of doing. Motivation determines what you do. Attitude determines how well you do it.

—LOU HOLTZ

True success is overcoming the fear of being unsuccessful.

—PAUL SWEENEY

If at first you do succeed—try to hide your astonishment.

—Los Angeles Times Syndicate

If you're not failing now and again, it's a sign you're playing it safe.

—WOODY ALLEN

You're never as good as everyone tells you when you win, and you're never as bad as they say when you lose.

—LOU HOLTZ WITH JOHN HEISLER
The Fighting Spirit

It takes as much courage to have tried and failed as it does to have tried and succeeded.

—ANNE MORROW LINDBERGH

It isn't failing that spells one's downfall; it's running away, giving up.

—MICHEL GRECO

If at first you don't succeed, try, try again. Then give up. There's no use in being a damn fool about it.

—W. C. FIELDS

Being defeated is often a temporary condition. Giving up is what makes it permanent.

—MARILYN VOS SAVANT

On this earth, in the final analysis, each of us gets exactly what he deserves. But only the successful recognise this.

—GEORGES SIMENON

If at first you don't succeed, you are running about average.

—M. H. ALDERSON

Success is not forever, and failure's not fatal.

—DON SHULA WITH KEN BLANCHARD
Everyone's a Coach

Failure is an event, never a person.

—WILLIAM D. BROWN
Welcome Stress!

Do not let what you cannot do interfere with what you can do.

—JOHN WOODEN
They Call Me Coach

Defeat may serve as well as victory to shake the soul and let the glory out.

—EDWIN MARKHAM

Failure doesn't hurt you. It's the fear of failure that's the killer.

—JACK LEMMON
quoted by Mike Bygrave in *You*

THE REWARD FOR WORK WELL DONE . . .

The reward for work well done is the opportunity to do more.

—JONAS SALK, MD

The reward of a thing well done is to have done it.

—RALPH WALDO EMERSON

Work is something you can count on, a trusted, lifelong friend who never deserts you.

—MARGARET BOURKE-WHITE

The biggest mistake you can make is to believe that you are working for someone else.

—*Bits & Pieces*

The work praises the man.

—IRISH PROVERB

One of the greatest sources of energy is pride in what you are doing.

—*SPOKES*

Do the best you can in every task, no matter how unimportant it may seem at the time. No one learns more about a problem than the person at the bottom.

—SANDRA DAY O'CONNOR

Manual labour to my father was not only good and decent for its own sake but, as he was given to saying, it straightened out one's thoughts.

—MARY ELLEN CHASE
A Goodly Fellowship

Just as there are no little people or unimportant lives, there is no insignificant work.

—ELENA BONNER
Alone Together

There's no labour a man can do that's undignified—if he does it right.

—BILL COSBY

Happiness, I have discovered, is nearly always a rebound from hard work.

—DAVID GRAYSON
Adventures in Contentment

Look at a day when you are supremely satisfied at the end. It's not a day when you lounge around doing nothing. It's when you've had everything to do, and you've done it.

—MARGARET THATCHER

There are no menial jobs, only menial attitudes.

—WILLIAM J. BENNETT
The Book of Virtues

There is a kind of victory in good work, no matter how humble.

—JACK KEMP

Thinking is the hardest work there is, which is probably the reason so few engage in it.

—HENRY FORD

Ability will never catch up with the demand for it.

—MALCOLM S. FORBES

Accomplishments have no colour.

—LEONTYNE PRICE

The best preparation for work is not thinking about work, talking about work, or studying for work: it is work.

—WILLIAM WELD

The more I want to get something done, the less I call it work.

—RICHARD BACH
*Illusions: The Adventures
of a Reluctant Messiah*

Nothing is work unless you'd rather be doing something else.

—GEORGE HALAS

My father always told me, "Find a job you love and you'll never have to work a day in your life."

—JIM FOX

When we do the best that we can, we never know what miracle is wrought in our life or in the life of another.

—HELEN KELLER

What you have inherited from your fathers, earn over again for yourselves, or it will not be yours.

—JOHANN WOLFGANG VON GOETHE

Blessed is the person who is too busy to worry in the daytime and too sleepy to worry at night.

—LEO AIKMAN
in *Journal-Constitution*
(Atlanta, Georgia)

Not only is woman's work never done, the definition keeps changing.

—BILL COPELAND
in *Herald-Tribune* (Sarasota, Florida)

We work to become, not to acquire.

—ELBERT HUBBARD

It is enterprise which builds and improves the world's possessions. If enterprise is afoot, wealth accumulates whatever may be happening to thrift; and if enterprise is asleep, wealth decays whatever thrift may be doing.

—JOHN MAYNARD KEYNES
A Treatise on Money

Perfection is finally attained, not when there is no longer anything to add, but when there is no longer anything to take away.

—ANTOINE DE SAINT-EXUPÉRY

If you have a job without any aggravations, you don't have a job.

—MALCOLM S. FORBES

Work keeps us from three evils: boredom, vice and need.

—VOLTAIRE

Retirement, we understand, is great if you are busy, rich and healthy. But then, under those conditions, work is great too.

—BILL VAUGHAN

It's strange how unimportant your job is when you're asking for a raise, but how important it can be when you want to take a day off.

—EARL A. MATHES
in *Tri-County Record* (Kiel, Wisconsin)

I don't know what liberation can do about it, but even when the man helps, woman's work is never done.

—BERYL PFIZER

There is no such thing as a non-working mother.

—HESTER MUNDIS
Powermom

Work consists of whatever a body is obliged to do, and play consists of whatever a body is not obliged to do.

—MARK TWAIN
The Adventures of Tom Sawyer

Retirement should be based on the tread, not the mileage.

—ALLEN LUDDEN

I don't want to achieve immortality through my work. I want to achieve immortality through not dying.

—WOODY ALLEN

It proves, on close examination, that work is less boring than amusing oneself.

—CHARLES BAUDELAIRE

EVERYWHERE IS WALKING DISTANCE . . .

Everywhere is walking distance if you have the time.

—STEVEN WRIGHT

The perfect journey is circular— the joy of departure and the joy of return.

—DINO BASILI
in *Il Tempe* (Rome, Italy)

What is travelling? Changing your place? By no means! Travelling is changing your opinions and your prejudices.

—ANATOLE FRANCE

The world is a book, and those who do not travel read only one page.

—ST. AUGUSTINE

There ain't no surer way to find out whether you like people or hate them than to travel with them.

—MARK TWAIN

The rule for travelling abroad is to take our common sense with us, and leave our prejudices behind.

—WILLIAM HAZLITT

Travelling is like falling in love; the world is made new.

—JAN MYRDAL

A good traveller is one who does not know where he is going. A perfect traveller does not know where he came from.

—LIN YUTANG

Be careful going in search of adventure—it's ridiculously easy to find.

—WILLIAM LEAST HEAT MOON
Blue Highways: A Journey into America

Most travel is best of all in the anticipation or the remembering; the reality has more to do with losing your luggage.

—REGINA NADELSON
in *European Travel & Life*

The average tourist wants to go to places where there are no tourists.

—SAM EWING

Men travel faster now, but I do not know if they go to better things.

—WILLA CATHER
Death Comes for the Archbishop

Each year it seems to take less time to fly across the ocean and longer to drive to work.

—*The Globe and Mail* (Toronto, Ontario)

For travel to be delightful, one must have a good place to leave and return to.

—FREDERICK B. WILCOX

THE ART OF CONVERSATION

"

Words can sometimes, in moments of grace, attain the quality of deeds.

—ELIE WIESEL

"

IT'S A STRANGE WORLD OF LANGUAGE . . .

It's a strange world of language in which skating on thin ice can get you into hot water.

—FRANKLIN P. JONES
in *Quote*

If the English language made any sense, lackadaisical would have something to do with a shortage of flowers.

—DOUG LARSON

Words are vehicles that can transport us from the drab sands to the dazzling stars.

—M. ROBERT SYME

Words are like diamonds. Polish them too much, and all you get are pebbles.

—BRYCE COURTENAY

All words are pegs to hang ideas on.

—HENRY WARD BEECHER

Words can sometimes, in moments of grace, attain the quality of deeds.

—ELIE WIESEL

Words without ideas are like sails without wind.

—*Courier-Record*
(Blackstone, Virginia)

A cliché is only something well said in the first place.

—BILL GRANGER
There Are No Spies

To "coin a phrase" is to place some value upon it.

—E. H. EVENSON

A different language is a different vision of life.

—FEDERICO FELLINI

Learn a new language and get a new soul.

—CZECH PROVERB

He who does not know foreign languages does not know anything about his own.

—JOHANN WOLFGANG VON GOETHE

It is often wonderful how putting down on paper a clear statement of a case helps one to see, not perhaps the way out, but the way in.

—A. C. BENSON

In certain trying circumstances, urgent circumstances, desperate circumstances, profanity furnishes a relief denied even to prayer.

—MARK TWAIN

Mincing your words makes it easier if you have to eat them later.

—FRANKLIN P. JONES

The two words "information" and "communication" are often used interchangeably, but they signify quite different things. Information is giving out; communication is getting through.

—SYDNEY J. HARRIS

Man does not live by words alone, despite the fact that sometimes he has to eat them.

—ADLAI STEVENSON

When a man eats his words, that's recyling.

—FRANK A. CLARK

By inflection you can say much more than your words do.

—MALCOLM S. FORBES

Brevity may be the soul of wit, but not when someone's saying, "I love you."

—JUDITH VIORST

A spoken word is not a sparrow. Once it flies out, you can't catch it.

—RUSSIAN PROVERB

Be careful of your thoughts; they may become words at any moment.

—IARA GASSEN

Words, once they're printed, have a life of their own.

—CAROL BURNETT

Everything becomes a little different as soon as it is spoken out loud.

—HERMANN HESSE

If you wouldn't write it and sign it, don't say it.

—EARL WILSON

Among my most prized possessions are words that I have never spoken.

—ORSON REGA CARD

Words are as beautiful as wild horses, and sometimes as difficult to corral.

—TED BERKMAN
in *Christian Science Monitor*

Look out how you use proud words. When you let proud words go, it is not easy to call them back.

—CARL SANDBURG
Slabs of the Sunburnt West

Words of comfort, skilfully administered, are the oldest therapy known to man.

—LOUIS NIZER

If you would be pungent, be brief; for it is with words as with sunbeams. The more they are condensed, the deeper they burn.

—ROBERT SOUTHEY

You can suffocate a thought by expressing it with too many words.

—Frank A. Clark

If it takes a lot of words to say what you have in mind, give it more thought.

—Dennis Roth

Say what you have to say, not what you ought.

—Henry David Thoreau

Why doesn't the fellow who says "I'm no speechmaker" let it go at that instead of giving a demonstration?

—Kin Hubbard

The reason we make a long story short is so that we can tell another.

—Sharon Shoemaker

The most valuable of all talents is that of never using two words when one will do.

—Thomas Jefferson

It's all right to hold a conversation, but you should let go of it now and then.

—Richard Armour

To speak of "mere words" is much like speaking of "mere dynamite."

—C. J. Ducasse
in *The Key Reporter*

To base thought only on speech is to try nailing whispers to the wall. Writing freezes thought and offers it up for inspection.

—Jack Rosenthal
in *New York Times Magazine*

When the mouth stumbles, it is worse than the foot.

—West African proverb

One way to prevent conversation from being boring is to say the wrong thing.

—Frank Sheed

The first requirement of good conversation is that nobody should know what is coming next.

—Havilah Babcock

Conversation means being able to disagree and still continue the discussion.

—Dwight MacDonald

Candour is a compliment; it implies equality. It's how true friends talk.

—Peggy Noonan
What I Saw at the Revolution

The genius of communication is the ability to be both totally honest and totally kind at the same time.

—John Powell

Fine words butter no parsnips.

—English proverb

Words must surely be counted among the most powerful drugs man ever invented.

—LEO ROSTEN

Sticks and stones may break our bones, but words will break our hearts.

—ROBERT FULGHUM
All I Really Need to Know I Learned in Kindergarten

The bitterest tears shed over graves are for words left unsaid and deeds left undone.

—HARRIET BEECHER STOWE

Do not the most moving moments of our lives find us all without words?

—MARCEL MARCEAU

In prayer it is better to have a heart without words than words without a heart.

—JOHN BUNYAN

Sometimes good intentions and feelings are of greater moment than the awkwardness of their expression.

—JONATHAN YARDLEY

It is a damned poor mind indeed that can't think of at least two ways of spelling any word.

—ANDREW JACKSON

Too much agreement kills a chat.

—ELDRIDGE CLEAVER
Soul on Ice

To touch a child's face, a dog's smooth coat, a petaled flower, the rough surface of a rock is to set up new orders of brain motion. To touch is to communicate.

—JAMES W. ANGELL
Yes Is a World

What a wonderful thing is the mail, capable of conveying across continents a warm human hand-clasp.

—Quoted by Ranjan Bakshi

A letter is a soliloquy, but a letter with a postscript is a conversation.

—LIN YUTANG

There is nothing like sealing a letter to inspire a fresh thought.

—AL BERNSTEIN

Parents can plant magic in a child's mind through certain words spoken with some thrilling quality of voice, some uplift of the heart and spirit.

—ROBERT MacNEIL
Wordstruck

A pun is a pistol let off at the ear; not a feather to tickle the intellect.

—CHARLES LAMB

SKILFUL LISTENING IS THE BEST REMEDY . . .

Skilful listening is the best remedy for loneliness, loquaciousness and laryngitis.
—WILLIAM ARTHUR WARD
in *Tribune*
(San Diego, California)

The greatest gift you can give another is the purity of your attention.
—RICHARD MOSS, MD

Listening, not imitation, may be the sincerest form of flattery.
—JOYCE BROTHERS

There is no greater loan than a sympathetic ear.
—FRANK TYGER
in *National Enquirer*

In order that all men may be taught to speak truth, it is necessary that all likewise should learn to hear it.
—SAMUEL JOHNSON

Good communication is as stimulating as black coffee, and just as hard to sleep after.
—ANNE MORROW LINDBERGH
Gift from the Sea

The less you talk, the more you're listened to.
—ABIGAIL VAN BUREN

Talk to a man about himself and he will listen for hours.
—BENJAMIN DISRAELI

Give every man thy ear but few thy voice.
—WILLIAM SHAKESPEARE

The most important thing in communication is to hear what isn't being said.
—PETER F. DRUCKER

There is always hope when people are forced to listen to both sides.
—JOHN STUART MILL

A good listener is not only popular everywhere, but after a while he knows something.
—WILSON MIZNER

Listen, or thy tongue will keep thee deaf.
—NATIVE AMERICAN PROVERB

No one really listens to anyone else. Try it for a while, and you'll see why.
—MIGNON McLAUGHLIN

To entertain some people all you have to do is listen.
—BERNARD EDINGER

Two great talkers will not travel far together.
—SPANISH PROVERB

Listening to both sides of a story will convince you that there is more to a story than both sides.

—FRANK TYGER

Sainthood emerges when you can listen to someone's tale of woe and not respond with a description of your own.

—ANDREW V. MASON, MD

Most people would rather defend to the death your right to say it than listen to it.

—ROBERT BRAULT

SILENCES MAKE THE REAL CONVERSATIONS . . .

Silences make the real conversations between friends. Not the saying but the never needing to say is what counts.

—MARGARET LEE RUNBECK
Answer Without Ceasing

Hospitality consists in a little fire, a little food and an immense quiet.

—RALPH WALDO EMERSON

In quiet places, reason abounds.

—ADLAI E. STEVENSON

Well-timed silence is the most commanding expression.

—MARK HELPRIN
in *The Wall Street Journal*

There are times when silence has the loudest voice.

—LEROY BROWNLOW
Today Is Mine

The time to stop talking is when the other person nods his head affirmatively but says nothing.

—HENRY S. HASKINS
Meditations in Wall Street

The right word may be effective, but no word was ever as effective as a rightly timed pause.

—MARK TWAIN

He approaches nearest to the gods who knows how to be silent, even though he is in the right.

—CATO

Silence is one of the hardest arguments to refute.

—JOSH BILLINGS

Silence, along with modesty, is a great aid to conversation.

—MONTAIGNE

Silence is the safety zone of conversation.

—ARNOLD H. GLASOW

Silence is still a marvellous language that has few initiates.

—ROGER DUHAMEL
Lettres à une Provinciale

Silence is the unbearable repartee.
—G. K. CHESTERTON

The most difficult thing in the world is to know how to do a thing and to watch someone else doing it wrong, without comment.
—THEODORE H. WHITE
in *The Atlantic*

Tact is the rare ability to keep silent while two friends are arguing, and you know both of them are wrong.
—HUGH ALLEN

Fools live to regret their words, wise men to regret their silence.
—WILL HENRY

Some people talk because they think sound is more manageable than silence.
—MARGARET HALSEY

If you reveal your secrets to the wind, you should not blame the wind for revealing them to the trees.
—KAHLIL GIBRAN
Sand and Foam

Blessed are they who have nothing to say and who cannot be persuaded to say it.
—JAMES RUSSELL LOWELL

If you really want to keep a secret you don't need any help.
—O. A. CARPING

Isn't it strange that we talk least about the things we think about most!
—CHARLES A. LINDBERGH

A secret is what you tell someone else not to tell because you can't keep it to yourself.
—LEONARD LOUIS LEVINSON

The vanity of being known to be entrusted with a secret is generally one of the chief motives to disclose it.
—SAMUEL JOHNSON

None are so fond of secrets as those who do not mean to keep them.
—C. C. COLTON

The knowledge that a secret exists is half of the secret.
—JOSHUA MEYROWITZ
No Sense of Place

He who has a secret should not only hide it, but hide that he has it to hide.
—THOMAS CARLYLE

No one keeps a secret better than he who ignores it.
—LOUIS-N. FORTIN

Another person's secret is like another person's money: you are not as careful with it as you are with your own.

—E. W. HOWE

Have you noticed that these days even a moment of silence has to be accompanied by background music?

—*Funny Funny World*

My personal hobbies are reading, listening to music and silence.

—EDITH SITWELL

I like the silent church before the service begins better than any preaching.

—RALPH WALDO EMERSON

BY EXPERT OPINION . . .

You can't always go by expert opinion. A turkey, if you ask a turkey, should be stuffed with grasshoppers, grit and worms.

—*Changing Times*

The man who never alters his opinion is like standing water, and breeds reptiles of the mind.

—WILLIAM BLAKE

Opinions should be formed with great caution—and changed with greater.

—JOSH BILLINGS

A leading authority is anyone who has guessed right more than once.

—FRANK A. CLARK

It is only about things that do not interest one that one can give a really unbiased opinion, which is no doubt the reason why an unbiased opinion is always valueless.

—OSCAR WILDE

We tolerate differences of opinion in people who are familiar to us. But differences of opinion in people we do not know sound like heresy or plots.

—BROOKS ATKINSON

The function of the expert is not to be more right than other people, but to be wrong for more sophisticated reasons.

—DAVID BUTLER

An expert is someone called in at the last minute to share the blame.

—SAM EWING
in *Mature Living*

Even when the experts all agree, they may well be mistaken.

—BERTRAND RUSSELL
The Skeptical Essays

The fewer the facts, the stronger the opinion.

—ARNOLD H. GLASOW

Every man has a right to be wrong in his opinions. But no man has a right to be wrong in his facts.

—BERNARD BARUCH
The Public Years

It is easy enough to hold an opinion, but hard work to actually know what one is talking about.

—PAUL F. FORD
Companion to Narnia

Too often we enjoy the comfort of opinion without the discomfort of thought.

—JOHN F. KENNEDY

The only thing worse than an expert is someone who thinks he's an expert.

—ALY A. COLON

A public-opinion poll is no substitute for thought.

—WARREN BUFFETT

Public opinion is like the castle ghost; no one has ever seen it, but everyone is scared of it.

—SIGMUND GRAFF

Every conviction was a whim at birth.

—HEYWOOD BROUN

Every new opinion, at its starting, is precisely in a minority of one.

—THOMAS CARLYLE

Refusing to have an opinion is a way of having one, isn't it?

—LUIGI PIRANDELLO
Each in His Own Way

Saying what we think gives a wider range of conversation than saying what we know.

—CULLEN HIGHTOWER

To disagree, one doesn't have to be disagreeable.

—BARRY M. GOLDWATER WITH JACK CASSERLY
Goldwater

There's a difference between opinion and conviction. My opinion is something that is true for me personally; my conviction is something that is true for everybody—in my opinion.

—SYLVIA CORDWOOD

ADMIRABLE ADVICE . . .

I sometimes give myself admirable advice, but I am incapable of taking it.

—MARY WORTLEY MONTAGU

To profit from good advice requires more wisdom than to give it.

—JOHN CHURTON COLLINS

Advice is an uncertain gift.

—WHITNEY JEFFERY

You don't need to take a person's advice to make him feel good—just ask for it.

—Laurence J. Peter
Peter's Almanac

Advice is what we ask for when we already know the answer but wish we didn't.

—Erica Jong

A knife of the keenest steel requires the whetstone, and the wisest man needs advice.

—Zoroaster

Expert advice is a great comfort, even when it's wrong.

—Quoted by Ellen Currie
in *The New York Times*

When we ask for advice, we are usually looking for an accomplice.

—Marquis de La Grange

Most of us ask for advice when we know the answer but want a different one.

—Ivern Ball
in *National Enquirer*

Good advice usually works best when preceded by a bad scare.

—Al Batt

When we are well, we all have good advice for those who are ill.

—Terence

Of the few innocent pleasures left to men past middle life, the jamming of common sense down the throats of fools is perhaps the keenest.

—T. H. Huxley

We are never so generous as when giving advice.

—François de La Rochefoucauld

People who have what they want are fond of telling people who haven't what they want that they really don't want it.

—Ogden Nash

We give advice by the bucket but take it by the grain.

—William Alger

The thing to do with good advice is to pass it on. It is never any good to oneself.

—Oscar Wilde

Advice should always be consumed between two thick slices of doubt.

—Walt Schmidt
in *Parklabrea News*

Don't be troubled if the temptation to give advice is irresistible; the ability to ignore it is universal.

—*Planned Security*

The best advice yet given is that you don't have to take it.

—LIBBIE FUDIM

USE SOFT WORDS . . .

Use soft words and hard arguments.

—ENGLISH PROVERB

A good indignation makes an excellent speech.

—RALPH WALDO EMERSON

There is nothing in the world like a persuasive speech to fuddle the mental apparatus.

—MARK TWAIN

If you have an important point to make, don't try to be subtle or clever. Use a pile driver. Hit the point once. Then come back and hit it again. Then hit it a third time a tremendous whack.

—WINSTON CHURCHILL

Charm is a way of getting the answer yes without asking a clear question.

—ALBERT CAMUS
The Fall

Praise, like gold and diamonds, owes its value only to its scarcity.

—SAMUEL JOHNSON

Sandwich every bit of criticism between two layers of praise.

—MARY KAY ASH
Mary Kay on People Management

Example is not the main thing in influencing others. It is the only thing.

—ALBERT SCHWEITZER

THE GREAT CHARM IN ARGUMENT . . .

The great charm in argument is really finding one's own opinions, not other people's.

—EVELYN WAUGH

Charm is the enchanted dart, light and subtle as a hummingbird. But it is deceptive in one thing: like a sense of humour, if you think you've got it, you probably haven't.

—LAURIE LEE
I Can't Stay Long

It is better to debate a question without settling it than to settle a question without debating it.

—JOSEPH JOUBERT

Nothing can keep an argument going like two persons who aren't sure what they're arguing about.

—O. A. BATTISTA

A single fact will often spoil an interesting argument.
—*Selected Cryptograms III*

You have not converted a man because you have silenced him.
—John Morley

It is impossible to defeat an ignorant man in an argument.
—William G. McAdoo

In quarrelling, the truth is always lost.
—Publilius Syrus

Never answer an angry word with an angry word. It's the second one that makes the quarrel.
—W. A. Nance

People generally quarrel because they cannot argue.
—G. K. Chesterton
More Quotable Chesterton

The difficult part in an argument is not to defend one's opinion but rather to know it.
—André Maurois

Quarrels would not last long if the fault were on one side only.
—François de La Rochefoucauld

Violence in the voice is often only the death rattle of reason in the throat.
—John F. Boyes

Whether on the road or in an argument, when you see red it's time to stop.
—Jan McKeithen

Anybody who thinks there aren't two sides to every argument is probably in one.
—*The Cockle Bur*

An apology is the superglue of life. It can repair just about anything.
—Lynn Johnston

The man who offers an insult writes it in sand, but for the man who receives it, it's chiseled in bronze.
—Giovanni Guareschi

An ounce of apology is worth a pound of loneliness.
—Joseph Joubert

An apology is a good way to have the last word.
—*Dell Crossword Puzzles*

PRAYER IS WHEN YOU TALK TO GOD . . .

Prayer is when you talk to God; meditation is when you listen to God.
—Quoted by Diana Robinson
in *The People's Almanac*

Prayer is the key of the morning and the bolt of the evening.
—MOHANDAS K. GANDHI

The greatest prayer is patience.
—GAUTAMA BUDDHA

What we usually pray to God is not that His will be done, but that He approve ours.
—HELGA BERGOLD GROSS

The object of most prayers is to wangle an advance on good intentions.
—ROBERT BRAULT

Certain thoughts are prayers. There are moments when, whatever be the attitude of the body, the soul is on its knees.
—VICTOR HUGO

If you begin to live life looking for the God that is all around you, every moment becomes a prayer.
—FRANK BIANCO

Our prayers are answered not when we are given what we ask but when we are challenged to be what we can be.
—MORRIS ADLER

Any concern too small to be turned into a prayer is too small to be made into a burden.
—CORRIE TEN BOOM
Clippings from My Notebook

If we could all hear one another's prayers, God might be relieved of some of his burden.
—ASHLEIGH BRILLIANT

Serving God is doing good to man. But praying is thought an easier service and is therefore more generally chosen.
—BENJAMIN FRANKLIN

God is like a mirror. The mirror never changes but everybody who looks at it sees something different.
—Quoted by RABBI HAROLD KUSHNER in *Ultimate Issues*

Prayer is less about changing the world than it is about changing ourselves.
—DAVID J. WOLPE
Teaching Your Children About God

Get down on your knees and thank God you are on your feet.
—IRISH PROVERB

Never trust someone who has to change his tone to ask something of the Lord.
—ROBERTA A. EVERETT

Call on God, but row away from the rocks.
—ROBERT M. YOUNG

Trust in God—but tie your camel tight.
—PERSIAN PROVERB

CIVILISATION'S GIFT

Civilisation is a movement and not a condition, a voyage and not a harbour.

—ARNOLD TOYNBEE

GREAT IDEAS NEED LANDING GEAR . . .

Great ideas need landing gear as well as wings.

—C. D. JACKSON

The history of mankind is the history of ideas.

—LUDWIG VON MISES
Socialism: An Economic and Sociological Analysis

A man is but a product of his thoughts; what he thinks, that he becomes.

—MOHANDAS K. GANDHI

An invasion of armies can be resisted, but not an idea whose time has come.

—VICTOR HUGO

It is useless to send armies against ideas.

—GEORG BRANDES

Good ideas are not adopted automatically. They must be driven into practice with courageous impatience.

—ADM. HYMAN G. RICKOVER

A cup is useful only when it is empty; and a mind that is filled with beliefs, with dogmas, with assertions, with quotations is really an uncreative mind.

—J. KRISHNAMURTI

The man with a new idea is a crank until the idea succeeds.

—MARK TWAIN

The greatest discovery of my generation is that a human being can alter his life by altering his attitude.

—WILLIAM JAMES

Thought is action in rehearsal.

—SIGMUND FREUD

Change your thoughts and you change your world.

—REV. NORMAN VINCENT PEALE

He who cannot change the very fabric of his thought will never be able to change reality.

—ANWAR EL-SADAT

The mind is its own place, and in itself can make a heaven of hell, a hell of heaven.

—JOHN MILTON

If most of us are ashamed of shabby clothes and shoddy furniture, let us be more ashamed of shabby ideas and shoddy philosophies.

—ALBERT EINSTEIN

Civilisation is a movement and not a condition, a voyage and not a harbour.

—ARNOLD TOYNBEE

Good thoughts bear good fruit,
bad thoughts bear bad fruit—and
man is his own gardener.

—JAMES ALLEN

Bring ideas in and entertain them
royally, for one of them may be
the king.

—MARK VAN DOREN

The test of a first-rate intelligence
is the ability to hold two opposed
ideas in the mind at the same
time, and still retain the ability
to function.

—F. SCOTT FITZGERALD

I like to have a man's knowledge,
comprehend more than one class
of topics, one row of shelves. I
like a man who likes to see a fine
barn as well as a good tragedy.

—RALPH WALDO EMERSON

Learning is not attained by
chance. It must be sought for
with ardour and attended to with
diligence.

—ABIGAIL ADAMS

What we learn with pleasure we
never forget.

—ALFRED MERCIER

Most people are willing to pay
more to be amused than to be
educated.

—ROBERT C. SAVAGE
Life Lessons

Education is not training but
rather the process that equips you
to entertain yourself, a friend and
an idea.

—WALLACE STERLING

Education is not the filling of a
pail, but the lighting of a fire.

—WILLIAM BUTLER YEATS

There are two ways of spreading
light: to be the candle or the
mirror that reflects it.

—EDITH WHARTON

An education is like a crumbling
building that needs constant
upkeep with repairs and additions.

—LOUIS DUDEK

A master can tell you what he
expects of you. A teacher, though,
awakens your own expectations.

—PATRICIA NEAL WITH RICHARD DENEUT
As I Am: An Autobiography

A great teacher never strives to
explain his vision—he simply
invites you to stand beside him
and see for yourself.

—REV. R. INMAN

If you would thoroughly know
anything, teach it to others.

—TRYON EDWARDS

To teach is to learn twice.

—JOSEPH JOUBERT

Good education is the essential foundation of a strong democracy.
—BARBARA BUSH
in a preface to *America's Country Schools* by Andrew Gulliford

Education is more than a luxury; it is a responsibility that society owes to itself.
—ROBIN COOK
Coma

Education is learning what you didn't even know you didn't know.
—DANIEL J. BOORSTIN
Democracy and Its Discontents

Without education, we are in a horrible and deadly danger of taking educated people seriously.
—G. K. CHESTERTON

It is not the business of science to inherit the earth, but to inherit the moral imagination; because without that, man and beliefs and science will perish together.
—JACOB BRONOWSKI

Science has made us gods even before we are worthy of being men.
—JEAN ROSTAND

An age is called Dark, not because the light fails to shine, but because people refuse to see it.
—JAMES A. MICHENER
Space

In every work of genius, we recognise our own rejected thoughts; they come back to us with a certain alienated majesty.
—RALPH WALDO EMERSON

If you are seeking creative ideas, go out walking. Angels whisper to a man when he goes for a walk.
—RAYMOND INMAN

An idea can turn to dust or magic, depending on the talent that rubs against it.
—WILLIAM BERNBACH

Be curious always! For knowledge will not acquire you; you must acquire it.
—SUDIE BACK

Curiosity is the wick in the candle of learning.
—WILLIAM A. WARD

The little I know, I owe to my ignorance.
—SACHA GUITRY

Curiosity is a willing, a proud, an eager confession of ignorance.
—S. LEONARD RUBINSTEIN
Writing: A Habit of Mind

A sense of curiosity is nature's original school of education.
—SMILEY BLANTON, MD
Love or Perish

The human mind is as driven to understand as the body is driven to survive.

—HUGH GILMORE
in *The Philadelphia Inquirer Magazine*

If a man had as many ideas during the day as he does when he has insomnia, he'd make a fortune.

—GRIFF NIBLACK
in *News* (Indianapolis, Indiana)

Ideas are like rabbits. You get a couple and learn how to handle them, and pretty soon you have a dozen.

—JOHN STEINBECK

All my best thoughts were stolen by the ancients.

—RALPH WALDO EMERSON

A new idea is delicate. It can be killed by a sneer or a yawn; it can be stabbed to death by a quip, and worried to death by a frown on the right man's brow.

—CHARLIE BROWER

Man's mind stretched to a new idea never goes back to its original dimensions.

—OLIVER WENDELL HOLMES

One should never spoil a good theory by explaining it.

—PETER MCARTHUR

Once a new idea springs into existence, it cannot be unthought. There is a sense of immortality in a new idea.

—EDWARD DE BONO
New Think: The Use of Lateral Thinking in the Generation of New Ideas

An open mind collects more riches than an open purse.

—WILL HENRY

A cold in the head causes less suffering than an idea.

—JULES RENARD

READING FURNISHES THE MIND . . .

Reading furnishes the mind only with materials of knowledge; it is thinking that makes what we read ours.

—JOHN LOCKE

Reading is to the mind what exercise is to the body.

—JOSEPH ADDISON

Books may well be the only true magic.

—ALICE HOFFMAN

Books are not made for furniture, but there is nothing else that so beautifully furnishes a house.

—HENRY WARD BEECHER

Reading makes immigrants of us all—it takes us away from home, but more important, it finds homes for us everywhere.

—HAZEL ROCHMAN
Against Borders

There are perhaps no days of our childhood we lived so fully as those we believe we left without having lived them: those we spent with a favourite book.

—MARCEL PROUST

From your parents you learn love and laughter and how to put one foot before the other. But when books are opened you discover that you have wings.

—HELEN HAYES WITH SANDFORD DODY
On Reflection

Books are the carriers of civilisation. Without books, history is silent, literature dumb, science crippled, thought and speculation at a standstill.

—BARBARA W. TUCHMAN

A great novel takes you deep into the wonders and complexities of other lives, freeing you from reality.

—SISTER WENDY BECKETT
Sister Wendy's Odyssey

Fiction reveals truths that reality obscures.

—JESSAMYN WEST

If you would understand your own age, read the works of fiction produced in it. People in disguise speak freely.

—ARTHUR HELPS
*Thoughts in the Cloister
and the Crowd*

Books are more than books. They are the life, the very heart and core of ages past, the reason why men lived and worked and died, the essence and quintessence of their lives.

—AMY LOWELL

There are no faster or firmer friendships than those between people who love the same books.

—IRVING STONE

Every man who knows how to read has it in his power to magnify, to multiply the ways in which he exists, to make his life full, significant and interesting.

—ALDOUS HUXLEY

No one ever really paid the price of a book—only the price of printing it.

—LOUIS I. KAHN

A truly good book is something as wildly natural and primitive, mysterious and marvellous, ambrosial and fertile as a fungus or a lichen.

—HENRY DAVID THOREAU

Reading without reflecting is like eating without digesting.

—EDMUND BURKE

I would rather be a poor man in a garret with plenty of books than a king who did not love reading.

—THOMAS BABINGTON MACAULAY

My test of a good novel is dreading to begin the last chapter.

—THOMAS HELM

A book is a success when people who haven't read it pretend they have.

—Los Angeles Times Syndicate

Once you can read, all worlds are open to you.

—SISTER WENDY BECKETT
Sister Wendy's Odyssey

I divide all readers into two classes: those who read to remember and those who read to forget.

—WILLIAM LYON PHELPS

The wise man reads both books and life itself.

—LIN YUTANG

The library is the temple of learning, and learning has liberated more people than all the wars in history.

—CARL ROWAN

A book should serve as the axe for the frozen sea within us.

—FRANZ KAFKA

The real purpose of books is to trap the mind into doing its own thinking.

—CHRISTOPHER MORLEY

Without libraries what have we? We have no past and no future.

—RAY BRADBURY

Perhaps no place in any community is so totally democratic as the town library. The only entrance requirement is interest.

—LADY BIRD JOHNSON

A well-composed book is a magic carpet on which we are wafted to a world that we cannot enter in any other way.

—CAROLINE GORDON
How to Read a Novel

You know you've read a good book when you turn the last page and feel a little as if you have lost a friend.

—PAUL SWEENEY

Books support us in our solitude and keep us from being a burden to ourselves.

—JEREMY COLLIER

There is a wonder in reading braille that the sighted will never know: to touch words and have them touch you back.

—JIM FIEBIG

Great literature is like a love affair: you lose your own self and blend with another sensibility. It liberates you from your ego.

—LORD GOWRIE

A book, tight shut, is but a block of paper.

—CHINESE PROVERB

A great book should leave you with many experiences and slightly exhausted at the end. You live several lives while reading it.

—WILLIAM STYRON

A truly great book should be read in youth, again in maturity and once more in old age, as a fine building should be seen by morning light, at noon and by moonlight.

—ROBERTSON DAVIES
The Enthusiasms of Robertson Davies

Poetry is language at its most distilled and most powerful.

—RITA DOVE

A poem begins in delight and ends in wisdom.

—ROBERT FROST

"Tell me what you read and I'll tell you who you are" is true enough, but I'd know you better if you told me what you reread.

—FRANÇOIS MAURIAC

When something can be read without effort, great effort has gone into its writing.

—ENRIQUE JARDIEL PONCELA

Wherever they burn books they will also, in the end, burn human beings.

—HEINRICH HEINE

You don't have to burn books to destroy a culture. Just get people to stop reading them.

—RAY BRADBURY

An author retains the singular distinction of being the only person who can remain a bore long after he is dead.

—SYDNEY J. HARRIS

For a man to become a poet he must be in love, or miserable.

—GEORGE GORDON, LORD BYRON

You don't have to suffer to be a poet. Adolescence is enough suffering for anyone.

—JOHN CIARDI

Poetry is an echo, asking a shadow to dance.

—CARL SANDBURG

In the end, the poem is not a thing we see; it is, rather, a light by which we may see—and what we see is life.

—ROBERT PENN WARREN

The difference between reality and fiction? Fiction has to make sense.

—TOM CLANCY

Choose an author as you choose a friend.

—WENTWORTH DILLON

Fable is more historical than fact, because fact tells us about one man and fable tells us about a million men.

—G. K. CHESTERTON

Let us read and let us dance— two amusements that will never do any harm to the world.

—VOLTAIRE

When you take stuff from one writer, it's plagiarism; but when you take it from many writers it's research.

—WILSON MIZNER

There's nothing to writing. All you do is sit down at a typewriter and open a vein.

—RED SMITH

When I want to read a novel, I write one.

—BENJAMIN DISRAELI

I cannot conceive how a novelist could fail to pity or love the smallest creation of his imagination; incomplete as these characters may be, they are the writer's bond with the real world, its suffering and heartbreak.

—GABRIELLE ROY
The Fragile Lights of Earth: Articles and Memories 1942–1970

ART IS A STAPLE, LIKE BREAD . . .

Art is a staple, like bread or wine or a warm coat in winter. Man's spirit grows hungry for art in the same way his stomach growls for food.

—IRVING STONE
Depths of Glory

Art is the signature of civilisation.

—BEVERLY SILLS

Art extends each man's short time on earth by carrying from man to man the whole complexity of other men's lifelong experience, with all its burdens, colours and flavour.

—ALEKSANDR SOLZHENITSYN
One Word of Truth . . .

Every fragment of song holds
a mirror to a past moment for
someone.
> —FANNY CRADOCK
> *War Comes to Castle Rising*

A room hung with pictures is a
room hung with thoughts.
> —SIR JOSHUA REYNOLDS

Anyone who says you can't see a
thought simply doesn't know art.
> —WYNETKA ANN REYNOLDS

No great artist ever sees things as
they really are. If he did, he
would cease to be an artist.
> —OSCAR WILDE

Art is the demonstration that the
ordinary is extraordinary.
> —AMÉDÉE OZENFANT
> *Foundations of Modern Art*

Art doesn't reproduce the visible
but rather makes it visible.
> —PAUL KLEE

It has been said that art is a tryst;
for the joy of it maker and
beholder meet.
> —KOJIRO TOMITA

Art is the only way to run away
without leaving home.
> —TWYLA THARP

Where words fail, music speaks.
> —HANS CHRISTIAN ANDERSEN

Half of art is knowing when to
stop.
> —ARTHUR WILLIAM RADFORD

The other arts persuade us, but
music takes us by surprise.
> —EDUARD HANSLICK

Without music, life is a journey
through a desert.
> —PAT CONROY
> *Beach Music*

Country music is three chords and
the truth.
> —HARLAN HOWARD

Music is the way our memories
sing to us across time.
> —LANCE MORROW
> in *Time*

After silence, that which comes
nearest to expressing the
inexpressible is music.
> —ALDOUS HUXLEY
> *Music at Night*
> *and Other Essays*

Music washes away from the soul
the dust of everyday life.
> —BERTHOLD AUERBACH

Music is the shorthand of emotion.
> —LEO TOLSTOY

Music is a higher revelation than
philosophy.
> —LUDWIG VAN BEETHOVEN

People who make music together cannot be enemies, at least not while the music lasts.

—Paul Hindemith

He who sings frightens away his ills.

—Miguel de Cervantes Saavedra

God respects me when I work, but he loves me when I sing.

—Rabindranath Tagore

If I may venture my own definition of a folk song, I should call it "an individual flowering on a common stem."

—Ralph Vaughn Williams

Learning music by reading about it is like making love by mail.

—Luciano Pavarotti

No one should be allowed to play the violin until he has mastered it.

—Jim Fiebig

Those move easiest who have learned to dance.

—Alexander Pope

The truest expression of a people is in its dances and its music. Bodies never lie.

—Agnes de Mille

Inside every man there is a poet who died young.

—Stephan Kanfer

There is no abstract art. You must always start with something. Afterwards you can remove all traces of reality.

—Pablo Picasso

Every artist was first an amateur.

—Ralph Waldo Emerson

Every musical masterpiece is always greater than any performance of it. You play it as well as you can but it's still there, better than you can make it.

—André Previn

All art, like all love, is rooted in heartache.

—Alfred Stieglitz

What art offers is space—a certain breathing room for the spirit.

—John Updike

More important than a work of art itself is what it will sow. Art can die, a painting can disappear. What counts is the seed.

—Joan Miró

Art is the triumph over chaos.

—John Cheever

What is art but a way of seeing?

—Thomas Berger
Being Invisible

Talent is a flame. Genius is a fire.

—Bern Williams

A great artist is never poor.
—Isak Dinesen (Karen Blixen)
Anecdotes of Destiny

No one can arrive from being talented alone. God gives talent; work transforms talent into genius.
—Anna Pavlova

Discipline is the refining fire by which talent becomes ability.
—Roy L. Smith

Perfectionism is the enemy of creation, as extreme self-solicitude is the enemy of well-being.
—John Updike
Odd Jobs

When love and skill work together, expect a masterpiece.
—John Ruskin

I created nothing; I invented nothing; I imagined nothing; I perverted nothing; I simply discovered drama in real life.
—Bernard Shaw

There's no need to believe what an artist says. Believe what he does; that's what counts.
—David Hockney

Every child is an artist. The problem is how to remain an artist once he grows up.
—Pablo Picasso

Really we create nothing. We merely plagiarise nature.
—Jean Baitaillon

The cinema has no boundary; it is a ribbon of dream.
—Orson Welles

Of course, there must be subtleties. Just make sure you make them obvious.
—Billy Wilder

It pays to be obvious, especially if you have a reputation for subtlety.
—Isaac Asimov
Foundation

Simplicity, carried to an extreme, becomes elegance.
—Jon Franklin
Writing for Story

It is only by introducing the young to great literature, drama and music, and to the excitement of great science that we open to them the possibilities that lie within the human spirit—enable them to see visions and dream dreams.
—Eric Anderson

Man creates culture and through culture creates himself.
—Pope John Paul II
in *Osservatore Romano*

THE NATURE OF LIFE

There is no distance on this earth as far away as yesterday.

—Robert Nathan

IN THE LONG ETERNITY
OF TIME . . .

It is easier to accept the message
of the stars than the message of
the salt desert. The stars speak of
man's insignificance in the long
eternity of time; the deserts speak
of his insignificance right now.
—EDWIN WAY TEALE

Eternity is a terrible thought. I
mean, where's it going to end?
—TOM STOPPARD

Forever is a long time, but not as
long as it was yesterday.
—DENNIS H'ORGNIES

Time is but the stream I go
a-fishing in.
—HENRY DAVID THOREAU

Time neither subtracts nor divides,
but adds at such a pace it seems
like multiplication.
—BOB TALBERT

The future is the past returning
through another gate.
—ARNOLD H. GLASOW

Snatching the eternal out of the
desperately fleeting is the great
magic trick of human existence.
—TENNESSEE WILLIAMS
in *The New York Times*

Time is a versatile performer.
It flies, marches on, heals all
wounds, runs out and will tell.
—FRANKLIN P. JONES

Time goes, you say? Ah, no! Alas,
Time stays, we go.
—AUSTIN DOBSON

Time marks us while we are
marking time.
—THEODORE ROETHKE
Straw for the Fire

Time wastes our bodies and our
wits, but we waste time, so we
are quits.
—*Verse and Worse*

In rivers, the water that you touch
is the last of what has passed and
the first of that which comes: so
with present time.
—LEONARDO DA VINCI

You don't get to choose how
you're going to die. Or when. You
can only decide how you're going
to live. Now.
—JOAN BAEZ

The feeling of being hurried is not
usually the result of living a full
life and having no time. It is,
rather, born of a vague fear that
we are wasting our life.
—ERIC HOFFER

Time is a rhythm. It comes and goes like the crackle of electricity in the brain or the gush of blood through the heart or the tide up the beach.

—LYALL WATSON
Supernature

How you spend your time is more important than how you spend your money. Money mistakes can be corrected, but time is gone forever.

—DAVID B. NORRIS

Those who make the worst use of their time are the first to complain of its shortness.

—JEAN DE LA BRUYÈRE

Half our life is spent trying to find something to do with the time we have rushed through life trying to save.

—WILL ROGERS

Today's greatest labour-saving device is tomorrow.

—TOM WILSON

Mañana is often the busiest day of the week.

—SPANISH PROVERB

One of these days is none of these days.

—HENRI TUBACH

By the streets of "by and by" one arrives at the house of "never."

—SPANISH PROVERB

Don't put off for tomorrow what you can do today, because if you enjoy it today you can do it again tomorrow.

—JAMES A. MICHENER

Nothing adds to a person's leisure time like doing things when they are supposed to be done.

—O. A. BATTISTA

For disappearing acts, it's hard to beat what happens to the eight hours supposedly left after eight of sleep and eight of work.

—DOUG LARSON

As if we could kill time without injuring eternity!

—HENRY DAVID THOREAU

A man who has to be punctually at a certain place at five o'clock has the whole afternoon ruined for him already.

—LIN YUTANG
The Importance of Living

The surest way to be late is to have plenty of time.

—LEO KENNEDY

Normal day, let me be aware of
the treasure you are.

—MARY JEAN IRION

Butterflies count not months but
moments, and yet have time
enough.

—RABINDRANATH TAGORE

Time, for all its smuggling in of
new problems, conspicuously
cancels others.

—CLARA WINSTON
in *The Massachusetts Review*

Time has a wonderful way of
weeding out the trivial.

—RICHARD BEN SAPIR
Quest

I still find each day too short for
all the thoughts I want to think,
all the walks I want to take, all
the books I want to read and all
the friends I want to see.

—JOHN BURROUGHS

Yesterday is experience.
Tomorrow is hope. Today is
getting from one to the other as
best we can.

—JOHN M. HENRY

You must have been warned
against letting the golden hours
slip by; but some of them are
golden only because we let them
slip by.

—JAMES M. BARRIE

We are tomorrow's past.

—MARY WEBB
Precious Bane

The present is the point at which
time touches eternity.

—C. S. LEWIS
Screwtape Letters

Life is uncharted territory. It
reveals its story one moment at
a time.

—LEO BUSCAGLIA
in *Executive Health Report*

I never think of the future. It
comes soon enough.

—ALBERT EINSTEIN

There is no distance on this earth
as far away as yesterday.

—ROBERT NATHAN
So Love Returns

The past is really almost as much
a work of the imagination as the
future.

—JESSAMYN WEST

He who believes that the past
cannot be changed has not yet
written his memoirs.

—TORVALD GAHLIN

There is a time to let things
happen and a time to make things
happen.

—HUGH PRATHER
Notes on Love and Courage

Every man regards his own life as the New Year's Eve of time.

—JEAN PAUL RICHTER

The best thing about the future is that it comes only one day at a time.

—DEAN ACHESON

Life is not dated merely by years. Events are sometimes the best calendars.

—BENJAMIN DISRAELI

Time has no divisions to mark its passage; there is never a thunderstorm to announce the beginning of a new year. It is only we mortals who ring bells and fire off pistols.

—THOMAS MANN

Life is not a "brief candle." It is a splendid torch that I want to make burn as brightly as possible before handing it on to future generations.

—BERNARD SHAW

ALL THE ART OF LIVING . . .

All the art of living lies in a fine mingling of letting go and holding on.

—HAVELOCK ELLIS

God asks no man whether he will accept life. That is not the choice. One must take it. The only choice is how.

—HENRY WARD BEECHER

If we live good lives, the times are also good. As we are, such are the times.

—ST. AUGUSTINE

We are here to add what we can to, not to get what we can from, life.

—SIR WILLIAM OSLER

Presence is more than just being there.

—MALCOLM S. FORBES
The Further Sayings of Chairman Malcolm

There are three things that if a man does not know, he cannot live long in this world: what is too much for him, what is too little for him and what is just right for him.

—SWAHILI PROVERB

Besides the noble art of getting things done, there is the noble art of leaving things undone. The wisdom of life consists in the elimination of non-essentials.

—LIN YUTANG

You only live once. But if you
work it right, once is enough.
—FRED ALLEN

There is more to life than
increasing its speed.
—MOHANDAS K. GANDHI

Everything should be made as
simple as possible, but not
simpler.
—ALBERT EINSTEIN

I believe the art of living consists
not so much in complicating
simple things as in simplifying
things that are not.
—FRANÇOIS HERTEL

Simplicity is making the journey
of this life with just baggage
enough.
—CHARLES DUDLEY WARNER

Seize from every moment its
unique novelty, and do not
prepare your joys.
—ANDRÉ GIDE
Nourritures terrestres

A good cook is like a sorceress
who dispenses happiness.
—ELSA SCHIAPARELLI

There is no love sincerer than the
love of food.
—BERNARD SHAW

Excess on occasion is exhilarating.
It prevents moderation from
acquiring the deadening effect of
a habit.
—W. SOMERSET MAUGHAM

If you can spend a perfectly
useless afternoon in a perfectly
useless manner, you have learned
how to live.
—LIN YUTANG

He does not seem to me to be a
free man who does not sometimes
do nothing.
—CICERO

How we spend our days is, of
course, how we spend our lives.
—ANNIE DILLARD
The Writing Life

A holiday gives one a chance
to look backward and forward,
to reset oneself by an inner
compass.
—MAY SARTON
At Seventy (A Journal)

The time to relax is when you
don't have time for it.
—SYDNEY J. HARRIS

A vacation is having nothing to do
and all day to do it in.
—ROBERT ORBEN

The discovery of a new dish does more for human happiness than the discovery of a star.

—ANTHELME BRILLAT-SAVARIN

We never repent of having eaten too little.

—THOMAS JEFFERSON

One of the very nicest things about life is the way we must regularly stop whatever it is we are doing and devote our attention to eating.

—LUCIANO PAVAROTTI WITH WILLIAM WRIGHT
Pavarotti, My Own Story

There is a sufficiency in the world for man's need but not for man's greed.

—MOHANDAS K. GANDHI

Whatever will satisfy hunger is good food.

—CHINESE PROVERB

'Tis an ill cook that cannot lick his own fingers.

—WILLIAM SHAKESPEARE

One must ask children and birds how cherries and strawberries taste.

—JOHANN WOLFGANG VON GOETHE

Never eat more than you can lift.

—*Miss Piggy's Guide to Life,*
as told to Henry Beard

We are all mortal until the first kiss and the second glass of wine.

—EDUARDO GALEANO
The Book of Embraces

Be glad of life because it gives you the chance to love and to work and to play and to look up at the stars.

—HENRY VAN DYKE

The art of living is more like wrestling than dancing.

—MARCUS AURELIUS

Part of the art of living is knowing how to compare yourself with the right people. Dissatisfaction is often the result of unsuitable comparison.

—DR. HEINRICH SOBOTKA
Madame

Is not life a hundred times too short for us to bore ourselves?

—FRIEDRICH NIETZSCHE

Enjoy the little things, for one day you may look back and realise they were the big things.

—ROBERT BRAULT
in *National Enquirer*

Yes, there is a nirvana; it is in leading your sheep to a green pasture, and in putting your child to sleep, and in writing the last line of your poem.

—KAHLIL GIBRAN

When things start going your way, it's usually because you stopped going the wrong way down a one-way street.
—Los Angeles Times Syndicate

One ought, every day at least, to hear a little song, read a good poem, see a fine picture and, if possible, speak a few reasonable words.
—JOHANN WOLFGANG VON GOETHE

IDEALS ARE LIKE THE STARS . . .

Ideals are like the stars. We never reach them but, like the mariners on the sea, we chart our course by them.
—CARL SCHURZ

The ideals which have lighted my way, and time after time have given me new courage to face life cheerfully, have been kindness, beauty and truth.
—ALBERT EINSTEIN
Ideas and Opinions

When you teach your son, you teach your son's son.
—THE TALMUD

The true idealist pursues what his heart says is right in a way that his head says will work.
—RICHARD M. NIXON

If things were really as we wanted them to be, people would still complain that they were no longer what they used to be.
—PIERRE DAC

I am an idealist. I don't know where I'm going, but I'm on my way.
—CARL SANDBURG

SOME THINGS HAVE TO BE BELIEVED . . .

Some things have to be believed to be seen.
—RALPH HODGSON
The Skylark and Other Poems

One person with a belief is a social power equal to 99 who have only interests.
—JOHN STUART MILL

To believe with certainty, we must begin with doubting.
—STANISLAUS I

Faith is building on what you know is here, so you can reach what you know is there.
—CULLEN HIGHTOWER

Strike from mankind the principle of faith and men would have no more history than a flock of sheep.
—MARK BELTAIRE

Science is not only compatible
with spirituality; it is a profound
source of spirituality.

—CARL SAGAN
The Demon-Haunted World:
Science as a Candle in the Dark

If we were logical, the future
would be bleak indeed. But we
are more than logical. We are
human beings, and we have
faith, and we have hope, and
we can work.

—JACQUES COUSTEAU

We couldn't conceive of a miracle
if none had ever happened.

—LIBBIE FUDIM

In faith there is enough light for
those who want to believe and
enough shadows to blind those
who don't.

—BLAISE PASCAL

All I have seen teaches me to trust
the Creator for all I have not seen.

—RALPH WALDO EMERSON

Faith is knowing there is an ocean
because you have seen a brook.

—WILLIAM ARTHUR WARD

Faith is like radar that sees
through the fog—the reality of
things at a distance that the
human eye cannot see.

—CORRIE TEN BOOM
Tramp for the Lord

Faith is the bird that sings when
the dawn is still dark.

—RABINDRANATH TAGORE

What I admire in Columbus is not
his having discovered a world
but his having gone to search for
it on the faith of an opinion.

—A. ROBERT TURGOT

If the stars should appear just one
night in a thousand years, how
would men believe and adore!

—RALPH WALDO EMERSON

Many of us look at the Ten
Commandments as an exam
paper: eight only to be attempted.

—MALCOLM MUGGERIDGE
Reality Ireland

The finest fruit of serious learning
should be the ability to speak the
word God without reserve or
embarrassment.

—NATHAN M. PUSEY

Our rabbi once said, "God always
answers our prayers, it's just that
sometimes the answer is no."

—BARBARA FEINSTEIN

If you are not as close to God as
you used to be, who moved?

—*St. Matthias' Church Bulletin*

Sorrow looks back, worry looks
around, faith looks up.

—Quoted in *Guideposts Magazine*

It is good enough to talk of God while we are sitting here after a nice breakfast and looking forward to a nicer luncheon, but how am I to talk of God to the millions who have to go without two meals a day? To them God can only appear as bread and butter.

—Mohandas K. Gandhi

Real religion is a way of life, not a white cloak to be wrapped around us on the Sabbath and then cast aside into the six-day closet of unconcern.

—William Arthur Ward
Think It Over

Hope is the thing with feathers . . .

Hope is the thing with feathers that perches in the soul.

—Emily Dickinson

Hope smiles on the threshold of the year to come, whispering that it will be happier.

—Alfred, Lord Tennyson

He who has health has hope, and he who has hope has everything.

—Arab proverb

The natural flights of the human mind are not from pleasure to pleasure but from hope to hope.

—Samuel Johnson

Hope is not the conviction that something will turn out well but the certainty that something makes sense, regardless of how it turns out.

—Vaclav Havel
Disturbing the Peace

There is one thing which gives radiance to everything. It is the idea of something around the corner.

—G. K. Chesterton

Waiting is still an occupation. It is not having anything to wait for that is terrible.

—Cesare Pavese
Il Mestiere di Vivere

We must learn to reawaken and keep ourselves awake, not by mechanical aids, but by an infinite expectation of the dawn.

—Henry David Thoreau

In every winter's heart there is a quivering spring, and behind the veil of each night there is a smiling dawn.

—Kahlil Gibran

Sometimes our fate resembles a fruit tree in winter. Who would think that those branches would turn green again and blossom, but we hope it, we know it.

—Johann Wolfgang von Goethe

A ship should not ride on a single anchor, nor life on a single hope.

—Epictetus

We must accept finite disappointment, but we must never lose infinite hope.

—Rev. Martin Luther King Jr.

There are no hopeless situations; there are only people who have grown hopeless about them.

—Clare Boothe Luce

I have always been delighted at the prospect of a new day, a fresh try, one more start, with perhaps a bit of magic waiting somewhere behind the morning.

—J. B. Priestley

In the face of uncertainty, there is nothing wrong with hope.

—Bernie Siegel
Love, Medicine and Miracles

When you say a situation or a person is hopeless, you are slamming the door in the face of God.

—Rev. Charles L. Allen

There is no better or more blessed bondage than to be a prisoner of hope.

—Roy Z. Kemp

THE KIND OF BEAUTY I WANT . . .

The kind of beauty I want most is the hard-to-get kind that comes from within—strength, courage, dignity.

—Ruby Dee

Some people, no matter how old they get, never lose their beauty— they merely move it from their faces into their hearts.

—Martin Buxbaum
in *National Enquirer*

Love beauty; it is the shadow of God on the universe.

—Gabriela Mistral
Desolación

Though we travel the world over to find the beautiful, we must carry it with us or we find it not.

—Ralph Waldo Emerson

Taking joy in living is a woman's best cosmetic.

—Rosalind Russell

Tell a girl she's beautiful, and she wouldn't believe you really mean it. Tell her she's more beautiful than another girl, and she would delightfully believe you're being true.

—Hasna Hassan Sirajeddine

People have the strength to overcome their bodies. Their beauty is in their minds.

—PETER GABRIEL CLARK-BROWN
in *Style* magazine

It is amazing how complete is the delusion that beauty is goodness.

—LEO TOLSTOY

I'm tired of all this nonsense about beauty being only skin deep. That's deep enough. What do you want—an adorable pancreas?

—JEAN KERR
The Snake Has All the Lines

Nothing makes a woman more beautiful than the belief that she is beautiful.

—SOPHIA LOREN
Women & Beauty

Fashions fade; style is eternal.

—YVES SAINT LAURENT

The most beautiful thing we can experience is the mysterious. It is the source of all true art and science.

—ALBERT EINSTEIN

SPEAK THE TRUTH . . .

Speak the truth, but leave immediately after.

—SLOVENIAN PROVERB

Never assume the obvious is true.

—WILLIAM SAFIRE
Sleeper Spy

I have one request: may I never use my reason against truth.

—ELIE WIESEL
quoting from a Hasidic rabbi's prayer

Truth isn't always beauty, but the hunger for it is.

—NADINE GORDIMER

The truth is not always dressed for the evening.

—MARGARET LEWERTH
Stuyvesant Square

Truth has no special time of its own. Its hour is now—always.

—ALBERT SCHWEITZER
On the Edge of the Primeval Forest

Only the truth can still astonish people.

—JEAN-MARIE POUPART
Ma 'tite vache a mal aux pattes

Some people so treasure the truth that they use it with great economy.

—H. RAY GOLENOR

A half truth is a whole lie.

—YIDDISH PROVERB

A half-truth is usually less than half of that.

—BERN WILLIAMS

A truth that's told with bad intent
beats all the lies you can invent.
—WILLIAM BLAKE

The most dangerous untruths are
truths moderately distorted.
—GEORG CHRISTOPH LICHTENBERG

Add one small bit to the truth and
you inevitably subtract from it.
—*Dell Crossword Puzzles*

Many people today don't want
honest answers insofar as honest
means unpleasant or disturbing.
They want a soft answer that
turneth away anxiety.
—LOUIS KRONENBERGER

The man who is brutally honest
enjoys the brutality quite as much
as the honesty. Possibly more.
—RICHARD J. NEEDHAM
in *The Globe and Mail* (Toronto)

We have to live today by what
truth we can get today and
be ready tomorrow to call it
falsehood.
—WILLIAM JAMES

Truth is tough. It will not break,
like a bubble, at a touch. Nay,
you may kick it about all day,
and it will be round and
full at evening.
—OLIVER WENDELL HOLMES SR.

Most of the change we think we
see in life is due to truths being in
and out of favour.
—ROBERT FROST

Truth hurts—not the searching
after; the running from!
—JOHN EYBERG

The truth will ouch.
—ARNOLD H. GLASOW

Of course, it's the same old
story. Truth usually is the same
old story.
—MARGARET THATCHER

The colour of truth is grey.
—ANDRÉ GIDE

One of the most striking
differences between a cat and a
lie is that a cat has only nine lives.
—MARK TWAIN

A lie has speed, but truth has
endurance.
—EDGAR J. MOHN

Every time you try to smother a
truth, two others get their breath.
—BILL COPELAND

What upsets me is not that you
lied to me, but that from now on
I can no longer believe you.
—FRIEDRICH NIETZSCHE

He who mistrusts most should be trusted least.

—THEOGNIS

I seem to have been like a child playing on the sea shore, finding now and then a prettier shell than ordinary, whilst the great ocean of truth lay undiscovered before me.

—ISAAC NEWTON

A paradox is a truth that bites its own tale.

—*American Farm & Home Almanac*

We always weaken whatever we exaggerate.

—JEAN-FRANÇOIS DE LA HARPE

Nothing lays itself open to the charge of exaggeration more than the language of naked truth.

—JOSEPH CONRAD

Always tell the truth. You may make a hole in one when you're alone on the golf course someday.

—FRANKLIN P. JONES

It takes two to speak truth—one to speak and another to hear.

—HENRY DAVID THOREAU

We do not err because truth is difficult to see. It is visible at a glance. We err because this is more comfortable.

—ALEKSANDR SOLZHENITSYN

We lie loudest when we lie to ourselves.

—ERIC HOFFER

Men hate those to whom they have to lie.

—VICTOR HUGO

The most exhausting thing in life is being insincere.

—ANNE MORROW LINDBERGH
Gift from the Sea

HAPPINESS WALKS ON BUSY FEET

Happiness walks on busy feet.

—KITTE TURMELL

If only we'd stop trying to be happy, we could have a pretty good time.

—WILLARD R. ESPY

Man must search for what is right, and let happiness come on its own.

—JOHANN PESTALOZZI

Now and then it's good to pause in our pursuit of happiness and just be happy.

—Quoted in *The Cockle Bur*

Fortify yourself with contentment, for this is an impregnable fortress.

—EPICTETUS

To be without some of the things you want is an indispensable part of happiness.

—BERTRAND RUSSELL
The Conquest of Happiness

Before strongly desiring anything, we should look carefully into the happiness of its present owner.

—FRANÇOIS DE LA ROCHEFOUCAULD

It is an illusion to think that more comfort means more happiness. Happiness comes of the capacity to feel deeply, to enjoy simply, to think freely, to be needed.

—STORM JAMESON

Happiness in childhood, or adulthood for that matter, is sudden and unplanned: learning to balance a bike; damming a stream and sailing paper boats; catching a fish for the first time.

—MARTYN HARRIS
in *The Daily Telegraph*

Most people ask for happiness on condition. Happiness can be felt only if you don't set any conditions.

—ARTHUR RUBINSTEIN

Most men pursue pleasure with such breathless haste that they hurry past it.

—SÖREN KIERKEGAARD

The foolish person seeks happiness in the distance; the wise person grows it under his feet.

—JAMES OPPENHEIM

The discontented man finds no easy chair.

—BENJAMIN FRANKLIN

Real elation is when you feel you could touch a star without standing on tiptoe.

—DOUG LARSON

The more the heart is nourished with happiness, the more it is insatiable.

—GABRIELLE ROY

Joy seems to me a step beyond happiness—happiness is a sort of atmosphere you can live in sometimes when you're lucky. Joy is a light that fills you with hope and faith and love.

—ADELA ROGERS ST. JOHNS
Some Are Born Great

Happiness is good health and a bad memory.

—INGRID BERGMAN

The summit of happiness is reached when a person is ready to be what he is.

—ERASMUS

Don't wait around for other people to be happy for you. Any happiness you get you've got to make yourself.

—ALICE WALKER

Happiness is a thing to be practised, like the violin.

—JOHN LUBBOCK

One filled with joy preaches without preaching.

—MOTHER TERESA OF CALCUTTA

Happiness is a conscious choice, not an automatic response.

—MILDRED BARTHEL
in *Ensign*

Happiness often sneaks in through a door you didn't know you left open.

—JOHN BARRYMORE

To show a child what once delighted you, to find the child's delight added to your own—this is happiness.

—J. B. PRIESTLEY

Great joys, like griefs, are silent.

—SHACKERLEY MARMION

There can be no happiness if the things we believe in are different from the things we do.

—FREYA STARK
The Journey's Echo

Shared joy is double joy and shared sorrow is half-sorrow.

—SWEDISH PROVERB

Success is getting what you want. Happiness is liking what you get.

—H. JACKSON BROWN
A Father's Book of Wisdom

An ecstasy is a thing that will not go into words; it feels like music.

—MARK TWAIN

For happiness one needs security, but joy can spring like a flower even from the cliffs of despair.

—ANNE MORROW LINDBERGH

If you want others to be happy, practice compassion. If you want to be happy, practice compassion.

—DALAI LAMA

Unhappiness is the ultimate form of self-indulgence.

—TOM ROBBINS
Jitterbug Perfume

HUMOUR IS NOT A TRICK . . .

Humour is not a trick, not jokes. Humour is a presence in the world—like grace—and shines on everybody.

—GARRISON KEILLOR

Time spent laughing is time spent with the gods.

—JAPANESE PROVERB

Laughter is the shortest distance between two people.

—VICTOR BORGE

Wit surprises, humour illuminates.

—ELI SCHLEIFER

Laughter is the sun that drives winter from the human face.

—VICTOR HUGO

Laughter is a tranquilliser with no side effects.

—ARNOLD H. GLASOW

Like a welcome summer rain, humour may suddenly cleanse and cool the earth, the air and you.

—LANGSTON HUGHES
The Book of Negro Humor

Laughter is the brush that sweeps away the cobwebs of the heart.

—MORT WALKER

Laughter can be heard farther than weeping.

—YIDDISH PROVERB

Laughter translates into any language.

—*Graffiti*

The kind of humour I like is the thing that makes me laugh for five seconds and think for ten minutes.

—WILLIAM DAVIS

Good humour may be said to be one of the very best articles of dress one can wear in society.

—WILLIAM MAKEPEACE THACKERAY

Among those whom I like, I can find no common denominator; but among those whom I love, I can: all of them make me laugh.

—W. H. AUDEN

After God created the world, He made man and woman. Then, to keep the whole thing from collapsing, He invented humour.

—GUILLERMO MORDILLO

Imagination was given to man to compensate him for what he is not; a sense of humour, to console him for what he is.

—*The Wall Street Journal*

So many tangles in life are ultimately hopeless that we have no appropriate sword other than laughter.

—GORDON W. ALLPORT

It always hurts a bit when you strike your funny bone. That's the essence of humour.

—JIM FIEBIG

Someone who makes you laugh is a comedian. Someone who makes you think and then laugh is a humourist.

—GEORGE BURNS

We do have a zeal for laughter in most situations, give or take a dentist.

—JOSEPH HELLER

Nothing makes your sense of humour disappear faster than having somebody ask where it is.

—IVERN BALL
in *The Saturday Evening Post*

If you're going to be able to look back on something and laugh about it, you might as well laugh about it now.

—MARIE OSMOND

Anyone without a sense of humour is at the mercy of everyone else.

—WILLIAM ROTSLER

Beware of those who laugh at nothing or at everything.

—ARNOLD H. GLASOW

Next to power without honour, the most dangerous thing in the world is power without humour.

—ERIC SEVAREID

The love of truth lies at the root of much humour.

—ROBERTSON DAVIES
in *Our Living Tradition*

I think the next best thing to solving a problem is finding some humour in it.

—FRANK A. CLARK

Humour is a hole that lets the sawdust out of a stuffed shirt.

—JAN MCKEITHEN

Humour is laughing at what you haven't got when you ought to have it.

—LANGSTON HUGHES

A humourist is a fellow who realises, first, that he is no better than anybody else, and, second, that nobody else is either.

—HOMER MCLIN

Comedy has to be based on truth. You take the truth and you put a little curlicue at the end.

—SID CAESAR

Comedy is simply a funny way of being serious.

—PETER USTINOV

Always laugh at yourself first—before others do.

—ELSA MAXWELL
R.S.V.P.: Elsa Maxwell's Own Story

A laugh at your own expense costs you nothing.

—MARY H. WALDRIP
in *Advertiser* (Dawson County, Georgia)

Happy is the person who can laugh at himself. He will never cease to be amused.

—HABIB BOURGUIBA

Humour is a spontaneous, wonderful bit of an outburst that just comes. It's unbridled, it's unplanned, it's full of surprises.

—ERMA BOMBECK

Humour is a reminder that no matter how high the throne one sits on, one sits on one's bottom.

—TAKI

You cannot hold back a good laugh any more than you can the tide. Both are forces of nature.

—WILLIAM ROTSLER

The secret of life is to make people laugh.

—JOHN MORTIMER
in *Radio Times*

It has always seemed to me that hearty laughter is a good way to jog internally without having to go outdoors.

—NORMAN COUSINS
Anatomy of an Illness

When the first baby laughed for the first time, the laugh broke into a thousand pieces and they all went skipping about, and that was the beginning of fairies.

—JAMES M. BARRIE

No symphony orchestra ever played music like a two-year-old girl laughing with a puppy.

—BERN WILLIAMS
in *National Enquirer*

A pun is the lowest form of humour, unless you thought of it yourself.

—DOUG LARSON

WIT OUGHT TO BE A GLORIOUS TREAT . . .

Wit ought to be a glorious treat, like caviar. Never spread it about like marmalade.

—NOEL COWARD

Wit has truth in it; wisecracking is simply calisthenics with words.

—DOROTHY PARKER
in *The Paris Review*

Wit is the salt of conversation, not the food.

—WILLIAM HAZLITT

Wit is educated insolence.

—ARISTOTLE

A caricature is always true only for an instant.

—CHRISTIAN MORGENSTERN

Wit penetrates; humour envelops. Wit is a function of verbal intelligence; humour is imagination operating on good nature.

—PEGGY NOONAN
What I Saw at the Revolution

The wit of conversation consists more in finding it in others than in showing a great deal yourself.

—JEAN DE LA BRUYÈRE

THE ONLY WAY TO KEEP YOUR HEALTH . . .

The only way to keep your health is to eat what you don't want, drink what you don't like, and do what you'd druther not.

—MARK TWAIN

The only way for a rich man to be healthy is, by exercise and abstinence, to live as if he were poor.

—PAUL DUDLEY WHITE

So many people spend their health gaining wealth, and then have to spend their wealth to regain their health.

—A. J. REB MATERI
Our Family

It would be a service to mankind if the pill were available in slot machines and the cigarette were placed on prescription.

—MALCOLM POTTS, MD
in *The Observer* (London)

The best cure for hypochondria is to forget about your own body and get interested in someone else's.

—GOODMAN ACE

Those who think they have not time for bodily exercise will sooner or later have to find time for illness.

—EDWARD STANLEY

It is part of the cure to wish to be cured.

—SENECA

You know you've reached middle age when a doctor, not a policeman, tells you to slow down, all you exercise are your prerogatives and it takes you longer to rest than to get tired.

—*Friends News Sheet*
(Royal Perth Hospital, Australia)

An early-morning walk is a blessing for the whole day.

—Henry David Thoreau

As with liberty, the price of leanness is eternal vigilance.

—Gene Brown

Your body is the baggage you must carry through life. The more excess baggage, the shorter the trip.

—Arnold H. Glasow

You can't lose weight by talking about it. You have to keep your mouth shut.

—*The Old Farmer's Almanac*

You know it's time to diet when you push away from the table and the table moves.

—Quoted in *The Cockle Bur*

Probably nothing in the world arouses more false hopes than the first four hours of a diet.

—Dan Bennett

If it weren't for the fact that the TV set and the refrigerator are so far apart, some of us wouldn't get any exercise at all.

—Joey Adams

TAKING MY PROBLEMS ONE AT A TIME . . .

It's not easy taking my problems one at a time when they refuse to get in line.

—Ashleigh Brilliant

He who can't endure the bad will not live to see the good.

—Yiddish proverb

It has been my philosophy of life that difficulties vanish when faced boldly.

—Isaac Asimov
Foundation

When things are bad, we take comfort in the thought that they could always be worse. And when they are, we find hope in the thought that things are so bad they have to get better.

—Malcolm S. Forbes
The Sayings of Chairman Malcolm

I don't think of all the misery but of the beauty that still remains.

—Anne Frank
The Diary of a Young Girl

Although the world is full of suffering, it is also full of the overcoming of it.

—Helen Keller

Nothing is more desirable than to be released from an affliction, but nothing is more frightening than to be divested of a crutch.

—James Baldwin

A certain amount of opposition is a great help to a man. Kites rise against, not with the wind.

—John Neal

What I'm looking for is a blessing that's not in disguise.

—Kitty O'Neill Collins

People need resistance, for it is resistance which gives them their awareness of life.

—Karl Ritter

That some good can be derived from every event is a better proposition than that everything happens for the best, which it assuredly does not.

—James K. Feibleman

The worst thing in your life may contain seeds of the best. When you can see crisis as an opportunity, your life becomes not easier, but more satisfying.

—Joe Kogel

Storms make trees take deeper roots.

—Claude McDonald
in *The Christian Word*

Smooth seas do not make skilful sailors.

—African proverb

It is the wounded oyster that mends its shell with pearl.

—Ralph Waldo Emerson

The soul would have no rainbow had the eyes no tears.

—John Vance Cheney

Some people are always grumbling that roses have thorns; I am thankful that thorns have roses.

—Alphonse Karr

He knows not his own strength that hath not met adversity.

—Ben Jonson

Adversity is the trial of principle. Without it, a man hardly knows whether he is honest or not.

—Henry Fielding

You'll never find a better sparring partner than adversity.

—Walt Schmidt
in *Parklabrea News*
(Los Angeles)

A gem is not polished without rubbing, nor a man perfected without trials.

—Chinese proverb

Drag your thoughts away from your troubles—by the ears, by the heels, or any other way you can manage it. It's the healthiest thing a body can do.

—MARK TWAIN

Borrow trouble for yourself if that's your nature, but don't lend it to your neighbours.

—RUDYARD KIPLING
Rewards and Fairies

Don't meet trouble halfway. It is quite capable of making the entire journey.

—BOB EDWARDS

Simple solutions seldom are.

—*Forbes* magazine

No one has completed his education who has not learned to live with an insoluble problem.

—EDMUND J. KIEFER

Keep your face to the sunshine and you cannot see the shadows.

—HELEN KELLER

When you can't solve the problem, manage it.

—REV. ROBERT H. SCHULLER

Most problems precisely defined are already partially solved.

—HARRY LORAYNE
Memory Makes Money

If the only tool you have is a hammer, you tend to see every problem as a nail.

—ABRAHAM MASLOW

Nothing lasts forever—not even your troubles.

—ARNOLD H. GLASOW
in *Rotary "Scandal Sheet"*
(Graham, Texas)

People who drink to drown their sorrow should be told that sorrow knows how to swim.

—ANN LANDERS

The human capacity to fight back will always astonish doctors and philosophers. It seems, indeed, that there are no circumstances so bad and no obstacles so big that man cannot conquer them.

—JEAN TETREAU

How a person masters his fate is more important than what his fate is.

—WILHELM VON HUMBOLDT

All blessings are mixed blessings.

—JOHN UPDIKE

Most of the shadows of this life are caused by our standing in our own sunshine.

—RALPH WALDO EMERSON

Life would not be life if a sorrow
were sad, and a joy merry, from
beginning to end.
—GERMAINE GUÈVREMONT
En pleine terre

Untold suffering seldom is.
—FRANKLIN P. JONES

Night is the blotting paper for
many sorrows.
—LITAUISCH

The darkest hour has only
60 minutes.
—MORRIS MANDEL

When you get to the end of your
rope, tie a knot and hang on.
And swing!
—LEO BUSCAGLIA

Every problem contains within
itself the seeds of its own solution.
—EDWARD SOMERS in *National Enquirer*

Worry often gives a small thing a
big shadow.
—SWEDISH PROVERB

Little things console us because
little things afflict us.
—BLAISE PASCAL

For every problem there is one
solution which is simple, neat and
wrong.
—H. L. MENCKEN
A Mencken Chrestomathy

Inside every small problem is a
large problem struggling to get
out.
—PAUL HUGHES

People in distress will sometimes
prefer a problem that is familiar to
a solution that is not.
—NEIL POSTMAN

The first step in solving a problem
is to tell someone about it.
—JOHN PETER FLYNN

Some people suffer in silence
louder than others.
—MORRIE BRICKMAN

Never bear more than one kind of
trouble at a time. Some people
bear three—all they have had, all
they have now, and all they
expect to have.
—EDWARD EVERETT HALE

An adventure is an inconvenience
rightly considered. An
inconvenience is an adventure
wrongly considered.
—G. K. CHESTERTON

IT IS THE LOOSE ENDS . . .

It is the loose ends with which
men hang themselves.
—ZELDA FITZGERALD

Two dangers constantly threaten the world: order and disorder.

—PAUL VALÉRY

Nothing is really lost. It's just where it doesn't belong.

—SUZANNE MUELLER

One of the advantages of being disorderly is that one is constantly making exciting discoveries.

—A. A. MILNE

More things grow in the garden than the gardener sows.

—SPANISH PROVERB

Organising is what you do before you do something, so that when you do it, it's not all mixed up.

—A. A. MILNE

When one finds himself in a hole of his own making, it is a good time to examine the quality of workmanship.

—JON REMMERDE
in *The Christian Science Monitor*

WHEN LUCK ENTERS . . .

When luck enters, give him a seat!

—JEWISH PROVERB

A person often meets his destiny on the road he took to avoid it.

—JEAN DE LA FONTAINE

Fortune brings in some boats that are not steered.

—WILLIAM SHAKESPEARE

Heaven goes by favour. If it went by merit, you would stay out and your dog would go in.

—MARK TWAIN

It's hard to detect good luck—it looks so much like something you've earned.

—FRANK A. CLARK

Luck is the residue of design.

—BRANCH RICKEY

The luck of having talent is not enough; one must also have a talent for luck.

—HECTOR BERLIOZ

Luck never gives; it only lends.

—SWEDISH PROVERB

Good luck is with the man who doesn't include it in his plan.

—*Graffiti*

Thorough preparation makes its own luck.

—JOE POYER
The Contra

Luck is a matter of preparation meeting opportunity.

—OPRAH WINFREY

Miracles sometimes occur, but one has to work terribly hard for them.

—CHAIM WEIZMANN

Luck is not chance, it's toil. Fortune's expensive smile is earned.

—EMILY DICKINSON

One half of life is luck; the other half is discipline—and that's the important half, for without discipline you wouldn't know what to do with your luck.

—CARL ZUCKMAYER

With money in your pocket, you are wise and you are handsome and you sing well, too.

—YIDDISH PROVERB

Some people have all the luck. And they're the ones who never depend on it.

—BOB INGHAM

There is no substitute for incomprehensible good luck.

—LYNNE ALPERN AND ESTHER BLUMENFELD
Oh, Lord, I Sound Just Like Mama

Serendipity is looking in a haystack for a needle and discovering the farmer's daughter.

—Quoted by JULIUS H. COMROE JR.
in Retrospectroscope

It is an all-too-human frailty to suppose that a favourable wind will blow forever.

—RICK BODE
First You Have to Row a Little Boat

It is perhaps a more fortunate destiny to have a taste for collecting shells than to be born a millionaire.

—ROBERT LOUIS STEVENSON

Superstition is foolish, childish, primitive and irrational—but how much does it cost you to knock on wood?

—JUDITH VIORST
Love & Guilt & the Meaning of Life, Etc.

THE LIMITS OF THE POSSIBLE . . .

The only way of discovering the limits of the possible is to venture a little way past them into the impossible.

—ARTHUR C. CLARKE
Profiles of the Future

I have learned to use the word impossible with the greatest caution.

—WERNHER VON BRAUN

What we need are more people who specialise in the impossible.

—THEODORE ROETHKE

The difference between the impossible and the possible lies in a person's determination.

—TOMMY LASORDA

The impossible is often the untried.

—JIM GOODWIN

All things are possible until they are proved impossible—and even the impossible may only be so, as of now.

—PEARL S. BUCK
A Bridge for Passing

Progress begins with the belief that what is necessary is possible.

—NORMAN COUSINS

Start by doing what's necessary, then what's possible and suddenly you are doing the impossible.

—ST. FRANCIS OF ASSISI

Everything looks impossible for the people who never try anything.

—JEAN-LOUIS ETIENNE

The young do not know enough to be prudent, and therefore they attempt the impossible—and achieve it, generation after generation.

—PEARL S. BUCK

Nothing ever built arose to touch the skies unless some man dreamed that it should, some man believed that it could, and some man willed that it must.

—CHARLES F. KETTERING

Accomplishing the impossible means only that the boss will add it to your regular duties.

—DOUG LARSON

IF YOU WANT A PLACE IN THE SUN . . .

If you want a place in the sun, you've got to put up with a few blisters.

—ABIGAIL VAN BUREN

Always bear in mind that your own resolution to succeed is more important than any one thing.

—ABRAHAM LINCOLN

Probably the most honest "self-made man" ever was the one we heard say: "I got to the top the hard way—fighting my own laziness and ignorance every step of the way."

—JAMES THOM

You can't expect to make a place in the sun for yourself if you keep taking refuge under the family tree.

—CLAUDE McDONALD
in *The Christian Word*

The important thing in life is not to have a good hand but to play it well.

—LOUIS-N. FORTIN
Pensées, Proverbes, Maximes

Striving for success without hard work is like trying to harvest where you haven't planted.

—DAVID BLY
in *Desert News* (Salt Lake City)

Showing up is 80 per cent of life.

—WOODY ALLEN

If you play to win, as I do, the game never ends.

—STAN MIKITA
Journal (Edmonton, Alberta)

There are no secrets to success. It is the result of preparation, hard work, learning from failure.

—GEN. COLIN L. POWELL
in *The Black Collegian*

Success is how high you bounce when you hit bottom

—GEN. GEORGE S. PATTON

Success is often just an idea away.

—FRANK TYGER

Don't aim for success if you want it; just do what you love and believe in, and it will come naturally.

—DAVID FROST

Success is often the result of taking a misstep in the right direction.

—AL BERNSTEIN

Wherever you see a successful business, someone once made a courageous decision.

—PETER DRUCKER

The only thing that ever sat its way to success was a hen.

—SARAH BROWN

Success has a simple formula: do your best, and people may like it.

—SAM EWING

As a general rule, the most successful man in life is the man who has the best information.

—BENJAMIN DISRAELI

You're never a loser until you quit trying.

—MIKE DITKA

There's no secret about success. Did you ever know a successful man who didn't tell you about it?

—KIN HUBBARD

THE NATURAL WORLD

*When one tugs at a single thing in nature,
he finds it attached to the rest of the world.*

—John Muir

A FINE LANDSCAPE IS LIKE A PIECE OF MUSIC . . .

There is nothing like walking to get the feel of a country. A fine landscape is like a piece of music; it must be taken at the right tempo. Even a bicycle goes too fast.

—PAUL SCOTT MOWRER
The House of Europe

When one tugs at a single thing in nature, he finds it attached to the rest of the world.

—JOHN MUIR

The universe is not required to be in perfect harmony with human ambition.

—CARL SAGAN

Our Creator would never have made such lovely days and have given us the deep hearts to enjoy them unless we were meant to be immortal.

—NATHANIEL HAWTHORNE

Climb the mountains and get their good tidings. Nature's peace will flow into you as sunshine flows into trees. The winds will blow their freshness into you, and the storms their energy, while cares will drop off like falling leaves.

—JOHN MUIR

There is no silence like that of the mountains.

—GUY BUTLER
A Local Habitation

I have seen the sea when it is stormy and wild; when it is quiet and serene; when it is dark and moody. And in all its moods, I see myself.

—MARTIN BUXBAUM

I pray every day that God make me like a child, that is to say that he will let me see nature in the unprejudiced way that a child sees it.

—JEAN BAPTISTE CAMILLE COROT

Our Lord has written the promise of resurrection, not in books alone but in every leaf of springtime.

—MARTIN LUTHER

Spring hangs her infant blossoms on the trees / Rock'd in the cradle of the western breeze.

—WILLIAM COWPER

Spring, thy name is colour.

—LIBBIE FUDIM

Spring is when you feel like whistling even with a shoe full of slush.

—DOUG LARSON

Spring is nature's way of saying,
"Let's party!"

—Robin Williams

A little madness in the spring
is wholesome even for the king.

—Emily Dickinson

The first day of spring is one
thing, and the first spring day is
another. The difference between
them is sometimes as great as a
month.

—Henry Van Dyke

Summer afternoon—summer
afternoon; to me those have
always been the two most
beautiful words in the English
language.

—Henry James

Oh, the summer night has a smile
of light, and she sits on a sapphire
throne.

—B. W. Procter

A garden is the purest of human
pleasures; it is the greatest
refreshment to the spirits of man,
without which buildings and
palaces are but gross handiworks.

—Francis Bacon

Winter is not a season; it's an
occupation.

—Sinclair Lewis

For man, autumn is a time of
harvest, of gathering together.
For nature, it is a time of sowing,
of scattering abroad.

—Edwin Way Teale
Autumn Across America

Autumn is a second spring when
every leaf is a flower.

—Albert Camus

Autumn carries more gold in its
hand than all the other seasons.

—Jim Bishop

Autumn is a season followed
immediately by looking forward
to spring.

—Doug Larson

Few things are as democratic as a
snowstorm.

—Bern Williams
in *National Enquirer*

No winter lasts forever; no spring
skips its turn.

—Hal Borland
Sundial of the Seasons

I am sure it is a great mistake
always to know enough to go in
when it rains. One may keep snug
and dry by such knowledge, but
one misses a world of loveliness.

—Adeline Knapp

I like trees because they seem
more resigned to the way they
have to live than other things do.
—WILLA CATHER

All sunshine makes a desert.
—ARABIC PROVERB

When there is a river in your
growing up, you probably always
hear it.
—ANN ZWINGER
Run, River, Run

A man has made at least a start on
discovering the meaning of human
life when he plants shade trees
under which he knows full well
he will never sit.
—D. ELTON TRUEBLOOD

I never knew how soothing trees
are—many trees and patches of
open sunlight, and tree presences;
it is almost like having another
being.
—D. H. LAWRENCE

The soil in return for her service
keeps the tree tied to her, the
sky asks nothing and leaves
it free.
—RABINDRANATH TAGORE

He that plants trees loves others
besides himself.
—ENGLISH PROVERB

Everything is blooming most
recklessly; if it were voices instead
of colours, there would be an
unbelievable shrieking into the
heart of the night.
—RAINER MARIA RILKE
Letters of Rainer Maria Rilke

A woodland in full colour is
awesome as a forest fire; but a
single tree is like a dancing
tongue of flame to warm the
heart.
—HAL BORLAND
Sundial of the Seasons

Flowers always make people
better, happier and more helpful;
they are sunshine, food and
medicine to the soul.
—LUTHER BURBANK

If we had a keen vision of all that
is ordinary in human life, it would
be like hearing the grass grow or
the squirrel's heartbeat, and we
should die of that roar which is
the other side of silence.
—GEORGE ELIOT

The repetition in nature may
not be a mere recurrence. It may
be a theatrical "encore."
—G. K. CHESTERTON

I've always regarded nature as the
clothing of God.
—ALAN HOVHANESS

A bird does not sing because it has an answer. It sings because it has a song.

—CHINESE PROVERB

The Pyramids will not last a moment compared with the daisy.

—D. H. LAWRENCE
D. H. Lawrence and Italy

I don't ask for the meaning of the song of a bird or the rising of the sun on a misty morning. There they are, and they are beautiful.

—PETE HAMILL
in *Esquire*

Let us a little permit nature to take her own way; she better understands her own affairs than we.

—MONTAIGNE

One touch of nature makes the whole world kin.

—WILLIAM SHAKESPEARE

Repetition is the only form of permanence that nature can achieve.

—GEORGE SANTAYANA

If the human brain were so simple that we could understand it, we would be so simple that we couldn't.

—EMERSON M. PUGH

People from a planet without flowers would think we must be mad with joy the whole time to have such things about us.

—IRIS MURDOCH
A Fairly Honourable Defeat

The universe is merely a fleeting idea in God's mind—a pretty uncomfortable thought, particularly if you've just made a down payment on a house.

—WOODY ALLEN

I would rather live in a world where my life is surrounded by mystery than live in a world so small that my mind could comprehend it.

—HARRY EMERSON FOSDICK

Never a daisy grows but a mystery guides the growing.

—RICHARD REALF

Science cannot answer the deepest questions. As soon as you ask why there is something instead of nothing, you have gone beyond science. I find it quite improbable that such order came out of chaos. There has to be some organizing principle. God to me is the explanation for the miracle of existence—why there is something instead of nothing.

—ALLAN R. SANDAGE

Sometimes I think we're alone in the universe, and sometimes I think we're not. In either case, the idea is quite staggering.

—ARTHUR C. CLARKE

Unknowingly, we plough the dust of stars, blown about us by the wind, and drink the universe in a glass of rain.

—IHAB HASSAN

The universe is full of magical things patiently waiting for our wits to grow sharper.

—EDEN PHILLPOTTS
A Shadow Passes

If we do discover a complete theory about our lives and all existing things it should in time be understandable in broad principle to everyone, not just a few scientists. Then we shall all—philosophers, scientists, and just ordinary people—be able to take part in the discussion of the question of why it is that we and the universe exist. If we find the answer to that, it would be the ultimate triumph of human reason, for then we would know the mind of God.

—STEPHEN HAWKING
A Brief History of Time

Everybody wants to go back to nature—but not on foot.

—WERNER MITSCH

The sun, with all those planets revolving around it and dependent on it, can still ripen a bunch of grapes as if it had nothing else in the universe to do.

—GALILEO

To define the universe would be to contain it, and that would be to limit existence.

—DAVID BERESFORD
in *The Weekly Mail & Guardian*
(Johannesburg, South Africa)

The sky is the daily bread of the eyes.

—RALPH WALDO EMERSON

LEAVE A LANDSCAPE AS IT WAS . . .

There is nothing in which the birds differ more from man than the way in which they can build and yet leave a landscape as it was before.

—ROBERT LYND
The Blue Lion and Other Essays

Don't blow it—good planets are hard to find.

—Quoted in *Time*

It's a sobering thought that
animals prefer the stink of a
polecat to the scent of man.
—LAURENS VAN DER POST
in *Zulu Wilderness,* BBC1

What is the use of a house if you
haven't got a tolerable planet to
put it on?
—HENRY DAVID THOREAU

Growth for the sake of growth is
the ideology of the cancer cell.
—EDWARD ABBEY

Progress might have been all right
once, but it's gone on too long.
—OGDEN NASH

Progress is man's ability to
complicate simplicity.
—THOR HEYERDAHL
Fatu-Hiva

You can tell all you need to
about a society from how it treats
animals and beaches.
—FRANK DEFORD
in *Sports Illustrated*

Since the beginning each
generation has fought nature.
Now, in the life-span of a single
generation, we must turn around
180 degrees and become the
protector of nature.
—JACQUES-YVES COUSTEAU

We haven't got too much time left
to ensure that government of
the earth, by the earth, for
the earth, shall not perish from
the people.
—C. P. SNOW

The activist is not the man who
says the river is dirty. The activist
is the man who cleans up the
river.
—ROSS PEROT

Civilisation no longer needs to
open up wilderness; it needs
wilderness to open up the still
largely unexplored human mind.
—DAVID RAINS WALLACE
The Dark Range

If we do not permit the earth
to produce beauty and joy, it
will in the end not produce food
either.
—JOSEPH WOOD KRUTCH

A true conservationist is a man
who knows that the world is not
given by his fathers but borrowed
from his children.
—*John James Audubon*

I think God's going to come down
and pull civilisation over for
speeding.
—STEVEN WRIGHT

We abuse land because we regard it as a commodity belonging to us. When we see land as a community to which we belong, we may begin to use it with love and respect.

—ALDO LEOPOLD
A Sand County Almanac

The other planets may not be able to support life, but it isn't easy on this one either.

—*Banking*

Mud has been a strong factor in the shaping of New Zealand life. It has tried many hearts and broken some.

—ALAN MULGAN
Short History of New Zealand

THERE'S NO DEALING WITH A CAT . . .

There's no dealing with a cat who knows you're awake.

—BRAD SOLOMON
The Open Shadow

Ignorant people think it's the noise which fighting cats make that is so aggravating, but it ain't so; it's the sickening grammar they use.

—MARK TWAIN

The only mystery about the cat is why it ever decided to become a domestic animal.

—COMPTON MACKENZIE
Cats' Company

When dogs leap on to your bed, it's because they adore being with you. When cats leap on to your bed, it's because they adore your bed.

—ALISHA EVERETT

The cat could very well be man's best friend but would never stoop to admitting it.

—DOUG LARSON

Cats don't caress us—they caress themselves on us.

—RIVAROL

Cats have it all—admiration and an endless sleep and company only when they want it.

—ROD MCKUEN
Book of Days

You can keep a dog; but it is the cat who keeps people because cats find humans useful domestic animals. A dog will flatter you but you have to flatter a cat. A dog is an employee; the cat is a freelance.

—GEORGE MIKES
How to Be Decadent

Cats seem to go on the principle
that it never does any harm to ask
for what you want.

—JOSEPH WOOD KRUTCH
The Twelve Seasons

When I play with my cat, who
knows if I am not more of a
pastime to her than she is to me?

—MONTAIGNE

No matter how much cats fight,
there always seem to be plenty of
kittens.

—ABRAHAM LINCOLN

It is impossible to keep a straight
face in the presence of one or
more kittens.

—CYNTHIA E. VARNADO

You can't look at a sleeping cat
and be tense.

—JANE PAULEY

The idea of calm exists in a sitting
cat.

—JULES RENARD

Never try to outstubborn a cat.

—ROBERT A. HEINLEIN
The Notebooks of Lazarus Long

IF DOGS COULD TALK . . .

If dogs could talk, it would take a
lot of fun out of owning one.

—ANDREW A. ROONEY
Not That You Asked . . .

Dogs laugh, but they laugh with
their tails.

—MAX EASTMAN
Enjoyment of Laughter

One reason a dog can be such a
comfort when you're feeling blue
is that he doesn't try to find out
why.

—*National Enquirer*

To his dog, every man is
Napoleon; hence the popularity
of dogs.

—ALDOUS HUXLEY

The great pleasure of a dog is that
you may make a fool of yourself
with him and not only will he not
scold you, but he will make a fool
of himself too.

—SAMUEL BUTLER

The dog has got more fun out
of Man than Man has got
out of the dog, for the clearly
demonstrable reason that Man is
the more laughable of the two
animals.

—JAMES THURBER
Thurber's Dogs

A dog teaches a boy fidelity, perseverance, and to turn around three times before lying down.

—ROBERT BENCHLEY

There is no psychiatrist in the world like a puppy licking your face.

—BERN WILLIAMS

A dog wags its tail with its heart.

—MARTIN BUXBAUM
in *Table Talk*

Home computers are being called upon to perform many new functions, including the consumption of homework formerly eaten by the dog.

—DOUG LARSON

If you think dogs can't count, try putting three dog biscuits in your pocket and then giving Fido only two of them.

—PHIL PASTORET

Any time you think you have influence, try ordering around someone else's dog.

—*The Cockle Bur*

Door: What a dog is perpetually on the wrong side of.

—OGDEN NASH

We give them the love we can spare, the time we can spare. In return dogs have given us their absolute all. It is without a doubt the best deal man has ever made.

—ROGER CARAS
A Celebration of Dogs

THE WORLD OF NATIONS

To understand a man, you must know his memories. The same is true of a nation.

—ANTHONY QUAYLE

IN THE AUSTRALIAN DREAM . . .

In the Australian dream all the land is evenly beautiful, and beautifully even. Never too cold, never too hot, never uncomfortable in any way, really; just sunny.

—ROBIN BOYD
The Great Australian Dream

"Australianess" has always been the philosopher's stone, or poet's stone, of Australian culture. Every means has been tried in order to attain it.

—CLIVE JAMES
in *Times Literary Supplement*

Australians swallow more syllables than any other single item of consumption.

—SIR HERMANN BLACK
in *Sydney Morning Herald*

I suppose I should say coming *up* from Australia. I believe that absurdly shaped country lies right underneath the floor of one's coal cellar.

—OSCAR WILDE

Touch their hearts, and they laugh as they die for you.

—FRANCIS ADAMS
The Australians

Sport to many Australians is life and the rest a shadow.

—DONALD HORNE
The Lucky Country

Australia seems to produce more political cartoonists per head of population than any other country—probably a reflection of the ribald and iconoclastic nature of the average Australian.

—ROSS THOMSON AND BILL HEWISON

To be fair to Australians, they don't afford excessive respect to anybody. It's one of their virtues.

—MALCOLM MUGGERIDGE

Before the war who had ever heard of Anzac; hereafter who will ever forget it?

—PATSY ADAM-SMITH
The Anzacs

THERE IS NO SUCH THING AS A NORMAL ENGLISHMAN . . .

There is no such thing as a normal Englishman. It is only when we try to be normal that we give ourselves away.

—AUBERON WAUGH
in *The Daily Telegraph*

Britain is the grit in the European oyster.

—JOHN MAJOR

No country with cricket as one of its national games has ever become communist.

—WOODROW WYATT

Live as though you're going to die tomorrow and garden as though you will live forever.

—LIZA GODDARD

We English have sex on the brain, which is not the most satisfactory place for it.

—MALCOLM MUGGERIDGE
in *The Observer* (London)

Get pleasure from all the small things that you see—an animal, a flower, a tree—and you will have enjoyed the day to the best of your ability.

—BERYL REID
in *The Meaning of Life* (Virgin)

Convention is the damnation of progress. If you go down just one corridor of thinking, you never get to see what's in the side rooms.

—TREVOR BAYLISS
in *The Times*

When I started going to the cinema the only four-letter word there was "exit."

—SIR SYDNEY SAMUELSON

THE REAL ESSENCE OF CANADA . . .

To agree to disagree, to harness diversity, to respect dissent; perhaps this is the real essence of Canada.

—ROBERT L. PERRY
Peter's Quotations

The soul of Canada is a dual personality, and must remain only half-revealed to those who know only one language.

—FRANK OLIVER CALL
*Canadian Quotations
and Phrases*

Such a land [British Columbia] is good for an energetic man. It is also not so bad for the loafer.

—RUDYARD KIPLING

A Canadian is someone who drinks Brazilian coffee from an English teacup, and munches a French pastry while sitting on his Danish furniture, having just come home from an Italian movie in his German car. He picks up his Japanese pen and writes to his MP to complain about the American takeover of the Canadian publishing business.

—CAMPBELL HUGHES
in *Time*

"Liberty" sounds awkward on the Canadian tongue; we use "freedom," a more passive-sounding word. When I was a soldier applying for a three-day pass, I asked for "leave," a word that suggests permission. United States G.I.s were granted "liberty," a word that implies escape.

—PIERRE BERTON
Why We Act Like Canadians

Freedom is to you what the sun was for us. You take it for granted.

—MOHAMED MAGHJI
Vancouver Sun

THE AMERICAN DREAM IS NOT OVER . . .

The American dream is not over. America is an adventure.

—THEODORE WHITE

It is a part of the American character to consider nothing as desperate.

—THOMAS JEFFERSON

What is the essence of America? Finding and maintaining that perfect, delicate balance between freedom "to" and freedom "from."

—MARILYN VOS SAVANT
in *Parade*

America is a religious nation, but only because it is religiously tolerant and lets every citizen pray, or not pray, in his own way.

—From an editorial in
The New York Times

America is a place where Jewish merchants sell Zen love beads to agnostics for Christmas.

—JOHN BURTON BRIMER

The things that have made America great are being subverted for the things that make Americans rich.

—LOU ERICKSON

How often we fail to realise our good fortune in living in a country where happiness is more than a lack of tragedy.

—PAUL SWEENEY

America did not invent human rights. In a very real sense, it is the other way around. Human rights invented America.

—JIMMY CARTER

What the people want is very simple—they want an America as good as its promise.

—BARBARA JORDAN

LIBERTY IS ALWAYS DANGEROUS . . .

Liberty is always dangerous—but it is the safest thing we have.
—HARRY EMERSON FOSDICK

Liberty, when it begins to take root, is a plant of rapid growth.
—GEORGE WASHINGTON

Let freedom reign. The sun never set on so glorious a human achievement.
—NELSON MANDELA

Free is not the same as free and easy.
—LARRY EISENBERG

The cause of freedom, of the defense of man's conscience, is indivisible. By defending it in one country, we defend it everywhere in the world.
—VLADIMIR BUKOVSKY

Freedom is the right to be wrong, not the right to do wrong.
—JOHN G. DIEFENBAKER

Liberty is the only thing you cannot have unless you are willing to give it to others.
—WILLIAM ALLEN WHITE

There are two freedoms: the false where a man is free to do what he likes; the true where a man is free to do what he ought.
—CHARLES KINGSLEY

Your liberty to swing your arms ends where my nose begins.
—Quoted by STUART CHASE

The right to do something does not mean that doing it is right.
—WILLIAM SAFIRE
in *The New York Times*

My definition of a free society is a society where it is safe to be unpopular.
—ADLAI E. STEVENSON

Many politicians of our time are in the habit of laying down as self-evident the proposition that no people ought to be free until they are fit to use their freedom. The maxim is worthy of the fool in the old story, who had resolved not to go in the water until he had learnt to swim. If men are to wait for liberty until they become wise and good in slavery, they may indeed wait for ever.
—THOMAS BABINGTON MACAULAY, 1825

Freedom is like life. You cannot
be given life in instalments.
You cannot be given breath but
no body, nor a heart but no
blood vessels. Freedom is one
thing—you have it all or you are
not free.

> —DR. MARTIN LUTHER KING
> *A Testament of Hope,*
> *the Essential Writings*
> *of Martin Luther King, Jr.*

Freedom is a powerful animal that
fights the barriers, and sometimes
makes people wish for higher
fences.

> —LANCE MORROW
> in *Time*

The function of freedom is to free
somebody else.

> —TONI MORRISON

They have rights who dare defend
them.

> —ROGER BALDWIN

It is easy to take liberty for granted,
when you have never had it taken
from you.

> —DICK CHENEY

Those who expect to reap
the blessings of freedom
must undergo the fatigue of
supporting it.

> —THOMAS PAINE

Those who profess to favour
freedom and yet depreciate
agitation are men who want rain
without thunder and lightning.

> —FREDERICK DOUGLASS

Freedom never yet was given to
nations as a gift, but only as a
reward, bravely earned by one's
own exertions.

> —LAJOS KOSSUTH

The history of liberty is a history
of the limitation of government
power.

> —WOODROW WILSON

Loving someone else more than
yourself, that's freedom.

> —MALCOLM MUGGERIDGE
> in *Muggeridge*
> *Ancient and Modern*

The love of liberty is the love of
others. The love of power is the
love of ourselves.

> —WILLIAM HAZLITT

Freedom is nothing else but a
chance to be better.

> —ALBERT CAMUS
> *Resistance, Rebellion*
> *and Death*

Freedom is the right to choose the
habits that bind you.

> —RENATE RUBENSTEIN
> *Liefst Verliefd*

If a nation values anything more than freedom, it will lose its freedom; and the irony of it is that if it is comfort or money that it values more, it will lose that too.

—W. SOMERSET MAUGHAM
Strictly Personal

A country free enough to examine its own conscience is a land worth living in, a nation to be envied.

—H.R.H. PRINCE CHARLES

The clash of ideas is the sound of freedom.

—*Graffiti*

Where opinions, morals and politics are concerned, there is no such thing as objectivity. The best we can hope for is that freedom will enable subjective points of view to meet and complement each other.

—JEAN D'ORMESSON

A people that values its privileges above its principles soon loses both.

—DWIGHT D. EISENHOWER

If everything would be permitted to me, I would feel lost in this abyss of freedom.

—IGOR STRAVINSKY

No man is free who is not master of himself.

—EPICTETUS

It is a seldom-proferred argument as to the advantages of a free press that it has a major function in keeping the government itself informed as to what the government is doing.

—WALTER CRONKITE

A free press can be good or bad, but, most certainly, without freedom a press will never be anything but bad.

—ALBERT CAMUS

Where the press is free and every man able to read, all is safe.

—THOMAS JEFFERSON

Censorship reflects a society's lack of confidence in itself.

—POTTER STEWART

No woman can call herself free until she can choose consciously whether she will or will not be a mother.

—MARGARET SANGER

Freedom always carries a burden of proof, always throws us back on ourselves.

—SHELBY STEELE
The Content of Our Character

Every time we liberate a woman,
we liberate a man.

—MARGARET MEAD

Patriotism is not so much
protecting the land of our fathers
as preserving the land of our
children.

—JOSÉ ORTEGA Y GASSET

Freedom is the oxygen of the
soul.

—MOSHE DAYAN

Timid men prefer the calm of
despotism to the tempestuous sea
of liberty.

—THOMAS JEFFERSON

We are in bondage to the law
in order that we may be
free.

—CICERO

To live anywhere in the world
today and be against equality
because of race or colour is like
living in Alaska and being against
snow.

—WILLIAM FAULKNER
*Essays, Speeches
and Public Letters*

The defect of equality is that we
desire it only with our superiors.

—HENRY BECQUE

TO PREVENT INJUSTICE . . .

There may be times when
we are powerless to prevent
injustice, but there must never
be a time when we fail to
protest.

—ELIE WIESEL

History will have to record
that the greatest tragedy of this
period of social transition
was not the strident clamour
of the bad people, but the
appalling silence of the good
people.

—REV. MARTIN LUTHER KING JR.
Stride Toward Freedom

There is no happiness for
people at the expense of other
people.

—ANWAR EL-SADAT

Equal rights for the sexes
will be achieved only when
mediocre women occupy high
positions.

—FRANÇOISE GIROUD

Injustice anywhere is a threat to
justice everywhere.

—REV. MARTIN LUTHER KING JR.

To do injustice is more disgraceful
than to suffer it.

—PLATO

A great many people in this country are worried about law-and-order. And a great many people are worried about justice. But one thing is certain: you cannot have either until you have both.

—RAMSEY CLARK

In recognising the humanity of our fellow beings, we pay ourselves the highest tribute.

—THURGOOD MARSHALL

As long as you keep a person down, some part of you has to be down there to hold him down, so it means you cannot soar as you otherwise might.

—MARIAN ANDERSON

What is morally wrong cannot be politically right.

—WILLIAM GLADSTONE

One man cannot hold another man down in the ditch without remaining down in the ditch with him.

—BOOKER T. WASHINGTON

Justice may be blind, but she has very sophisticated listening devices.

—EDGAR ARGO
in *Funny Times*

Justice is the insurance we have on our lives, and obedience is the premium we pay for it.

—WILLIAM PENN

A minority group has "arrived" only when it has the right to produce some fools and scoundrels without the entire group paying for it.

—CARL T. ROWAN

We shall have to repent in this generation, not so much for the evil deeds of the wicked people, but for the appalling silence of the good people.

—REV. MARTIN LUTHER KING JR.

We are not bitter, not because we have forgiven but because there is so much to be done that we cannot afford to waste valuable time and resources on anger.

—GOVAN MBEKI
Johannesburg Weekly Mail

Until you can help your enemy and converse with him, until you can be of use to your fellow man, you have no human rights at all.

—YEHUDI MENUHIN

It is better to risk saving a guilty man than to condemn an innocent one.

—Voltaire

Most lawyers who win a case advise their clients that "we have won" and, when justice has frowned upon their cause, that "you have lost."

—Louis Nizer

Injustice is relatively easy to bear; what stings is justice.

—H. L. Mencken
Prejudices

That old law about "an eye for an eye" leaves everybody blind.

—Rev. Martin Luther King Jr.
Stride Toward Freedom

I would uphold the law if for no other reason but to protect myself.

—Thomas More

I sometimes wish that people would put a little more emphasis upon the observance of the law than they do upon its enforcement.

—Calvin Coolidge

The ultimate solution to the race problem lies in the willingness of men to obey the unenforceable.

—Rev. Martin Luther King Jr.

The worst form of injustice is pretended justice.

—Plato

THE REAL BEAUTY OF DEMOCRACY . . .

The real beauty of democracy is that the average man believes he is above average.

—Morrie Brickman

Man's capacity for justice makes democracy possible, but man's inclination to injustice makes democracy necessary.

—Reinhold Niebuhr

Democracy's real test lies in its respect for minority opinion.

—Ellery Sedgwick
in *Jersey Journal*

The test of courage comes when we are in the minority. The test of tolerance comes when we are in the majority.

—Ralph W. Sockman

Democracy without morality is impossible.

—Jack Kemp

Consensus means that lots of people say collectively what nobody believes individually.

—ABBA EBAN
in *Montreal Gazette*

Democracy means that if the doorbell rings in the early hours, it is likely to be the milkman.

—WINSTON CHURCHILL

Democracy does not guarantee equality, only equality of opportunity.

—IRVING KRISTOL

Democracy cannot survive without the guidance of a creative minority.

—HARLAN F. STONE

One has the right to be wrong in a democracy.

—CLAUDE PEPPER

Democracy is a small hard core of common agreement, surrounded by a rich variety of individual differences.

—JAMES B. CONANT

Our political institutions work remarkably well. They are designed to clang against each other. The noise is democracy at work.

—MICHAEL NOVAK

I like the noise of democracy.

—JAMES BUCHANAN

Democracy, like any noncoercive relationship, rests on a shared understanding of limits.

—ELIZABETH DREW
*Washington Journal:
The Events of 1973–1974*

People often say that, in a democracy, decisions are made by a majority of the people. Of course, that is not true. Decisions are made by a majority of those who make themselves heard and who vote—a very different thing.

—WALTER H. JUDD

Democracy is not a matter of sentiment, but of foresight. Any system that doesn't take the long run into account will burn itself out in the short run.

—CHARLES YOST

I'm tired of hearing it said that democracy doesn't work. Of course it doesn't work. We are supposed to work it.

—ALEXANDER WOOLLCOTT

Democracy, like love, can survive any attack—save neglect and indifference.

—PAUL SWEENEY

Every private citizen has a public responsibility.

—MYRA JANCO DANIELS
in *Newsweek*

The most important political office is that of private citizen.

—LOUIS BRANDEIS

Democracy is based upon the conviction that there are extraordinary possibilities in ordinary people.

—HARRY EMERSON FOSDICK

Sometimes a majority simply means that all the fools are on the same side.

—CLAUDE MCDONALD

Democracy is not a mathematical deduction proved once and for all time. Democracy is a just faith fervently held, a commitment to be tested again and again in the fiery furnace of history.

—JACK KEMP

Democracy may not prove in the long run to be as efficient as other forms of government, but it has one saving grace: it allows us to know and say that it isn't.

—BILL MOYERS
in *Newsweek*

There can be no daily democracy without daily citizenship.

—RALPH NADER

Democracy is like a raft. It won't sink, but you'll always have your feet wet.

—Quoted by RUSSELL LONG
in *The Washingtonian*

Whenever you find yourself on the side of the majority, it is time to pause and reflect.

—MARK TWAIN

It's not the voting that's democracy; it's the counting.

—TOM STOPPARD
Jumpers

Democracy is the only system that persists in asking the powers that be whether they are the powers that ought to be.

—SYDNEY J. HARRIS

In a democracy we have to be very firm in defending the right to speak, even for those whose views we find unacceptable.

—ARCHBISHOP DESMOND TUTU

Democracy is the recurrent suspicion that more than half of the people are right more than half of the time.

—E. B. WHITE
in *The New Yorker*

It's not the hand that signs the laws that holds the destiny of America. It's the hand that casts the ballot.

—HARRY S TRUMAN

Anything that keeps a politician humble is healthy for democracy.

—MICHAEL KINSLEY

Democracy is the art of disciplining oneself so that one need not be disciplined by others.

—GEORGES CLEMENCEAU

IN POLITICS . . .

In politics, what begins in fear usually ends in folly.

—SAMUEL TAYLOR COLERIDGE

I'm pretty good at soufflés, which is a politician's speciality after all—lots of hot air turned into confection.

—JACK STRAW

Politics are too serious a matter to be left to the politicians.

—GEN. CHARLES DE GAULLE

The bedfellows politics makes are never strange. It only seems that way to those who have not watched the courtship.

—KIRKPATRICK SALE

Politicians and journalists share the same fate in that they often understand tomorrow the things they talk about today.

—HELMUT SCHMIDT

Politics is like coaching a football team. You have to be smart enough to understand the game but not smart enough to lose interest.

—EUGENE MCCARTHY

No man should enter politics unless he is either independently rich or independently poor.

—ROBERT JAMES MANION
Gentlemen, Players and Politicians

A politician complaining about the media is like a sailor complaining about the sea.

—ENOCH POWELL

Politics is perhaps the only profession for which no preparation is thought necessary.

—ROBERT LOUIS STEVENSON

Politicians are like ships: noisiest when lost in a fog.

—BENNETT CERF

What's real in politics is what the voters decide is real.

—BEN J. WATTENBERG
Values Matter Most

The truly skilful politician is one who, when he comes to a fork in the road, goes both ways.

—MARCO A. ALMAZAN
Pildoras Anticonceptistas

Everything is changing. People are taking their comedians seriously and the politicians as a joke.

—WILL ROGERS

When the search for truth is confused with political advocacy, the pursuit of knowledge is reduced to the quest for power.

—ALSTON CHASE
In a Dark Wood

When things don't go well they like to blame presidents; and that's something that presidents are paid for.

—JOHN F. KENNEDY

Sincerity and competence is a strong combination. In politics, it's everything.

—PEGGY NOONAN
in *Catholic New York*

A statesman who keeps his ear permanently glued to the ground will have neither elegance of posture nor flexibility of movement.

—ABBA EBAN

When a man assumes a public trust he should consider himself as public property.

—THOMAS JEFFERSON

A perfect politician is a person who can lie to the press, then believe what he reads.

—WILL DURST

A strong conviction that something must be done is the parent of many bad measures.

—DANIEL WEBSTER

Those who corrupt the public mind are just as evil as those who steal from the public purse.

—ADLAI E. STEVENSON

Politicians say they're beefing up our economy. Most don't know beef from pork.

—HAROLD LOWMAN

Now and then an innocent man is sent to the legislature.

—KIN HUBBARD

We have a free press in Britain. Despite many occasions when we politicians find it intensely irritating, it is our good fortune that it is free. It keeps politicians honest and helps prevent corruption.

—MICHAEL PORTILLO

A politician without a prepared text is like a Boris Becker without a tennis racket, a dog biscuit without a dog, or opera glasses without an opera.

—C. M. BOWRA

When buying and selling are controlled by legislation, the first things to be bought and sold are legislators.

—P. J. O'ROURKE

Election year is that period when politicians get free speech mixed up with cheap talk.

—J. B. KIDD

A politician is a person who can make waves and then make you think he's the only one who can save the ship.

—IVERN BALL
in *Modern Secretary*

Politicians are people who, when they see light at the end of the tunnel, go out and buy some more tunnel.

—JOHN QUINTON

It's extremely difficult to build a political platform that supports candidates without holding up taxpayers.

—HAROLD COFFIN

Politics is the art of getting money from the rich and votes from the poor, with the pretext of protecting one from the other.

—*Muy Interesante*

Instead of giving a politician the keys to the city, it might be better to change the locks.

—DOUG LARSON

Washington is a place where politicians don't know which way is up and taxes don't know which way is down.

—ROBERT ORBEN
in *The Wall Street Journal*

To create a housing shortage in a huge country, heavily wooded, with a small population—ah, that's proof of pure political genius.

—RICHARD J. NEEDHAM
The Globe and Mail (Toronto)

IF A GOVERNMENT COMMISSION HAD WORKED ON THE HORSE . . .

If a government commission had worked on the horse, you would have had the first horse that could operate its knee joint in both directions. The only trouble is it couldn't have stood up.

—PETER DRUCKER

Bureaucracy is the art of making the possible impossible.

—JAVIER PASCUAL SALCEDO

I don't make jokes. I just watch the government and report the facts.

—WILL ROGERS

Governing a large country is like frying a small fish. You spoil it with too much poking.

—LAO-TZU

A little government and a little luck are necessary in life, but only a fool trusts either of them.

—P. J. O'ROURKE
Parliament of Whores

Everyone wants to live at the expense of the state. They forget that the state wants to live at the expense of everyone.

—FRÉDÉRIC BASTIAT

Government can't give us anything without depriving us of something else.

—HENRY HAZLITT
in *The Freeman*

Everybody wants to eat at the government's table, but nobody wants to do the dishes.

—WERNER FINCK

When government accepts responsibility for people, then people no longer take responsibility for themselves.

—GEORGE PATAKI

Useless laws weaken the necessary laws.

—MONTESQUIEU

A country is considered the more civilised the more the wisdom and efficiency of its laws hinder a weak man from becoming too weak or a powerful one too powerful.

—PRIMO LEVI
Survival In Auschwitz

You are better off not knowing how sausages and laws are made.

—Washington, D.C., adage

Government never furthered any enterprise but by the alacrity with which it got out of its way.

—HENRY DAVID THOREAU

A government is the only vessel known to leak from the top.

—JAMES RESTON
in *The New York Times*

Knowing exactly how much of the future can be introduced into the present is the secret of a great government.

—VICTOR HUGO

The best defence against usurpatory government is an assertive citizenry.

—WILLIAM F. BUCKLEY JR.
Windfall: The End of the Affair

Bad laws are the worst sort of tyranny.

—EDMUND BURKE

We should know everything we can about government—and the first thing we should know is what we're paying for it.

—ROBERT FULFORD
Financial Times

Government investigations have always contributed more to our amusement than they have to our knowledge.

—WILL ROGERS

What is the difference between a taxidermist and a tax collector? The taxidermist takes only your skin.

—MARK TWAIN

Tax reform is taking the taxes off things that have been taxed in the past and putting taxes on things that haven't been taxed before.

—ART BUCHWALD

The government deficit is the difference between the amount of money the government spends and the amount it has the nerve to collect.

—SAM EWING

FINANCE IS THE ART . . .

Finance is the art of passing currency from hand to hand until it finally disappears.

—ROBERT W. SARNOFF

There are three kinds of economist: those who can count and those who can't.

—EDDIE GEORGE

Money still talks, but it has to catch its breath more often.

—*Parts Pups*

Civilisations are remembered by their artefacts, not their bank rates.

—STEPHEN BAYLEY

Money talks—but credit has an echo.

—BOB THAVES

A big disappointment in life is the discovery that the man who writes the finance company ads isn't the one who makes the loans.

—*The London Free Press* (Ontario)

Time was when the average person could pay as he goes. Nowadays he has to pay as he comes and goes.

—O. A. Battista

An economist is an expert who will know tomorrow why the things he predicted yesterday didn't happen.

—Earl Wilson

Economics is extremely useful as a form of employment for economists.

—John Kenneth Galbraith

The economy depends about as much on economists as the weather does on weather forecasters.

—Jean-Paul Kauffmann

An economist's guess is liable to be just as good as anybody else's.

—Will Rogers

Isn't it strange? The same people who laugh at gypsy fortune-tellers take economists seriously.

—The Cincinnati Enquirer

The only function of economic forecasting is to make astrology look respectable.

—Ezra Solomon

We have become, to some extent, economic hypochondriacs. You get a wiggle in a statistic, and everyone runs to get the thermometer.

—Paul W. McCracken

Torture numbers, and they'll confess to anything.

—Gregg Easterbrook
in The New Republic

It is not the employer who pays— he only handles the money. It is the product that pays wages.

—Henry Ford

Although he may not always recognise his bondage, modern man lives under a tyranny of numbers.

—Nicholas Eberstadt
The Tyranny of Numbers:
Mismeasurement and Misrule

People have the wrong idea about money. They spend their lives chasing a myth—that the man with lots of it is happy by virtue of his wealth, and that people without money are unhappy. In doing so, they create a vision of something they want—realising later that, in fact, they don't want it. The only way to enjoy life is to keep one's needs simple.

—Sir John Moores
quoted in The Daily Telegraph

It would be nice if the poor were to get even half of the money that is spent in studying them.

—BILL VAUGHAN

To view poverty simply as an economic condition, to be measured by statistics, is simplistic, misleading and false; poverty is a state of mind, a matter of horizons.

—PATRICK J. BUCHANAN
Right from the Beginning

When economics gets important enough, it becomes political.

—PETER G. PETERSON

When goods do not cross borders, soldiers will.

—FRÉDÉRIC BASTIAT

There are so many men who can figure costs, and so few who can measure values.

—*Tribune* (San Marino, California)

Only a fool thinks price and value are the same.

—ANTONIO MACHADO

The best cure for the national economy would be economy.

—ASHLEY COOPER
in *News and Courier*
(Charleston, South Carolina)

Statistics are human beings with the tears wiped off.

—PAUL BRODEUR
Outrageous Misconduct

Money does make all the difference. If you have two jobs and you're rich, you have diversified interests. If you have two jobs and you're poor, you're moonlighting.

—*Changing Times*

People want economy, and they will pay any price to get it.

—LEE IACOCCA

The shortest recorded period of time lies between the minute you put some money away for a rainy day and the unexpected arrival of rain.

—JANE BRYANT QUINN

One thing I could never abide was the leaving of money to lie idle, or even to have credit and not use it.

—LORD THOMSON OF FLEET
After I Was Sixty

Measure wealth not by the things you have, but by the things you have for which you would not take money.

—ANONYMOUS

Money changes people just as
often as it changes hands.

—AL BATT

The most efficient labour-saving
device is still money.

—FRANKLIN P. JONES

Money is better than poverty, if
only for financial reasons.

—WOODY ALLEN

A rand goes a long way these
days. You can carry it around
for days without finding a thing it
will buy.

—*Daily Dispatch*
(East London, South Africa)

I don't like money, actually, but it
quiets my nerves.

—JOE LOUIS

Money is a good servant but a
bad master.

—FRENCH PROVERB

The beauty of having a low
income is that there is not enough
money to buy what you don't
really need.

—RAY INMAN

There is nothing so habit-forming
as money.

—DON MARQUIS

When a man says money can do
anything, that settles it; he hasn't
any.

—ED HOWE

Bankruptcy stared me in the face,
but one thought kept me calm;
soon I'd be too poor to need an
anti-theft alarm.

—GINA ROTHFELS

TO LIVE IN SOCIETY . . .

To live in society doesn't mean
simply living side by side with
others in a more or less close
cohesion; it means living through
one another and for one another.

—PAUL-EUGENE ROY

Civilisation is a process whose
purpose is to combine single
human individuals, and after that
families, and then races, peoples
and nations, into one great unity,
the unity of mankind.

—*The Complete Psychological
Works of Sigmund Freud*

We ought to think that we are
one of the leaves of a tree, and
the tree is all humanity. We
cannot live without the others,
without the tree.

—PABLO CASALS

A community is like a ship; everyone ought to be prepared to take the helm.

—Henrik Ibsen

If we cannot now end our differences, at least we can help make the world safe for diversity.

—John F. Kennedy

A school system without parents at its foundation is just like a bucket with a hole in it.

—Rev. Jesse L. Jackson

French statesman and winner of the Nobel Peace Prize: "In order to have peace we must want it, and not always doubt it."

—Aristide Briand
Quoted by Matthias Jaggi
in *Schweizer Jugend*

There's just no place you can go any longer and escape the global problems, so one's thinking must become global.

—Theodore Roszak

In every community, there is work to be done. In every nation, there are wounds to heal. In every heart, there is the power to do it.

—Marianne Williamson
A Return to Love

A nation is a body of people who have done great things together in the past and who hope to do great things together in the future.

—F. H. Underhill
*Colombo's Little Book
of Canadian Proverbs, Graffiti,
Limericks and Other Vital Matters*

No one is rich enough to do without a neighbour.

—Harold Helfer

I look to a time when brotherhood needs no publicity, to a time when a brotherhood award would be as ridiculous as an award for getting up each morning.

—Daniel D. Mich

We should see the new world order as a building constructed brick by brick and be motivated by the fact that we have only got as far as building the ground floor.

—Douglas Hurd
Daily Telegraph (London)

I can think of no more stirring symbol of man's humanity to man than a fire engine.

—Kurt Vonnegut

WHOEVER DOESN'T KNOW THE PAST . . .

Whoever doesn't know the past must have little understanding of the present and no vision of the future.

—JOSEPH S. RAYMOND

History is the unfolding of miscalculation.

—BARBARA TUCHMAN

History doesn't pass the dishes again.

—LOUIS-FERDINAND CÉLINE

History is a vast early-warning system.

—NORMAN COUSINS

History is a better guide than good intentions.

—JEANE J. KIRKPATRICK

Once the game is over, the king and the pawn go back into the same box.

—ITALIAN PROVERB

A nation forgetful and disrespectful of its past has no future, and deserves none.

—*Daily Telegraph* (London)

Righteousness is easy in retrospect.

—ARTHUR SCHLESINGER JR.
in *Newsweek*

Historians tend to be pessimists, for the only future they can imagine is the past.

—ROBERT SKIDELSKY

The history of every country begins in the heart of a man or a woman.

—WILLA CATHER

I look upon the whole world as my fatherland, and every war has to me the horror of a family feud.

—HELEN KELLER
in *New York Call*

To understand a man, you must know his memories. The same is true of a nation.

—ANTHONY QUAYLE

It was the same with those old birds in Greece and Rome as it is now. The only thing new in the world is the history you don't know.

—HARRY S TRUMAN

Genuine tragedies in the world are not conflicts between right and wrong. They are conflicts between two rights.

—GEORG HEGEL

Nationalism is an infantile disease. It is the measles of mankind.

—ALBERT EINSTEIN

In individuals, insanity is rare;
but in groups, parties, nations
and epochs, it is the rule.
—Friedrich Nietzsche

We have war when at least one
of the parties to a conflict wants
something more than it wants
peace.
—Jeane J. Kirkpatrick

In war, there are no unwounded
soldiers.
—José Narosky

The soldiers fight, and the kings
are heroes.
—Barbara Mechels

When elephants fight, it's the
grass that suffers.
—African proverb

Might does not make right; it only
makes history.
—Jim Fiebig

In war there is no second prize
for the runner-up.
—Gen. Omar N. Bradley

As long as war is regarded as
wicked, it will always have its
fascination. When it is looked
upon as vulgar, it will cease to be
popular.
—Oscar Wilde

You can build a throne with
bayonets, but you can't sit on it
for long.
—Boris Yeltsin

A peace which depends upon fear
is nothing but a suppressed war.
—Henry van Dyke

Foreign relations are like human
relations. They are endless. The
solution of one problem usually
leads to another.
—James Reston

Revolutions are built on empty
bellies.
—Wyndham Hartley
Natal Witness (South Africa)

Who overcomes by force hath
overcome but half his foe.
—John Milton

Perhaps the rediscovery of our
humanity, and the potential of the
human spirit which we have read
about in legends of older
civilisations, or in accounts of
solitary mystics, or in tales of
science fiction writers—perhaps
this will constitute the true
revolution of the future. The new
frontier lies not beyond the
planets but within each one of us.
—Pierre Elliott Trudeau
Biodynamics

A

Ability, 12, 16, 114, 116, 144
Abstinence, 164
Acceptance, 16, 22, 32, 95, 146, 149, 155
 of mistakes, 39, 61
 of truth, 14, 27, 40
Accidents, 16, 42, 45
Accomplishment, 13, 16, 21, 43, 70, 92, 112, 116
Accountability, 71
Acquisition, 13, 22, 71, 117, 136
Action, 64, 65, 66, 71, 94, 100 – 118
 delay of, 77, 110 – 111, 123
 goodness and, 42, 43, 49, 70, 77 – 79, 80, 81
Admiration, 49, 75, 78, 98, 180
 self -, 16, 24
Adolescence, 25, 53, 140
Adults, 25, 49, 57, 58, 60, 159
 children in, 26, 27, 28, 30, 68
Adventure, 36, 48, 118, 168
Adversity, 37, 64, 165 – 168
Advice, 59, 127, 128 – 129
Affection, 15, 16, 37, 47, 60
Affliction, 166, 168
Age, aging, 27 – 31, 34, 38, 55, 111
Agnostics, 186
Agreeability, 62
Airplanes, 69, 118
Amateurs, 143
Ambition, 20, 21, 174
America, Americans, 186, 195
Amusement, 39, 117, 135, 141, 163, 199
Angels, 41, 110, 136
Anger, 36, 74, 75, 86 – 88, 104, 191
Animals, 179
Annoyance, 69, 101
Answers, 40, 129, 130, 132, 153, 157

Anticipation, 23, 32, 118
Anzac, 184
Apathy, 86
Apologies, 70, 113, 131
Appearance, 24, 66
 aging and, 27, 29, 30
 reality vs., 16
Appetite, 88
Applause, 49, 89, 90
Apples, 49, 102
Appreciation, 51, 81
Approval, 24, 60, 132
April, 84
Ardour, 71, 135
Arguments, 90, 92, 122, 125, 126, 130, 131
Arithmetic, 61, 81
Armies, 134
Art of living, 25, 50, 52, 76, 149 – 152
Arts, 44, 141 – 144, 156
 study of, 60, 143
 visual, 44, 66, 103
Aspirations, 20
Astonishment, 58, 114, 156
Astrology, 84, 200
Attention, 98, 112, 124 – 125
Attitude, 69, 114, 116, 132, 134
Australia, Australians, 184
Authorities, 101, 112, 127
Autumn, 175
Awareness, 60, 148, 166

B

Babies, 58, 163
 birth of, 49, 54
Baggage, 118, 150, 165
Balance, 13, 23, 43, 71, 88
Bandwagon, 107
Bankruptcy, 202
Bargains, 51
Battle of the sexes, 52
Battles, 70
Beaches, 179

Beauty, 46, 54, 121, 152, 155 – 156, 179
 inner, 27, 29, 155
Bees, 23, 88, 93
Beginning, 102
Behaviour, 30, 37, 67, 78
Beliefs, 58, 60, 68, 69, 89, 92, 104, 134, 152 – 154, 160
Bells, 70, 89, 149
Bible, 46
Bigotry, 95
Biographies, 27, 109
Birds, 19, 21, 38, 103, 107, 151, 154, 177
Birth, 49, 54, 67
Birthdays, 20, 31
Birthplaces, 74
Bitterness, 75, 87, 123
Blame, 14, 27, 68, 80, 126, 127
Blessings, 81, 96, 103, 165, 166, 167
Blindness, 78, 153, 191
Bodies, 77, 92, 117, 132, 137, 143, 146, 156, 165
 aging of, 27, 29, 31
Boldness, 104 – 105, 110, 165
Bondage, 200
Bones, 58, 123
Books, 40, 59, 118, 137 – 141, 148
Bores, boredom, 72, 85, 90, 117, 122, 140, 151
Borrowing, 167
Brain, 84, 123, 177, 185
Bravery, 70, 76 – 77
Brevity, 120, 121, 122
Bridges, 22, 46, 79, 101, 112
Britain, 184, 185, 196
British Columbia, 185
Brotherhood, 203
Buildings, 19, 135, 140
Burdens, 41, 43, 94, 132, 139, 141, 189
Bureaucracy, 198
Burning, 41, 71, 84, 121, 140, 149

C

Calculation, 111
Calm, 181, 202
Calumny, 13
Camels, 43, 132
Canada, Canadians, 185 – 186
Cancer, 179
Candles, 12, 135, 136
Candour, 122
Capability, 64, 100
Carefulness, 111, 118, 121, 127
Caricature, 164
Caring, 36, 41, 81
Cats, 23, 34, 157, 180 – 181
Caution, 91, 111, 127
Censorship, 57, 189
Challenge, 132
Champagne, 62
Change, 13, 34, 53, 57, 68, 69,
  91, 102, 104, 118, 132, 148
  maturity and, 26
  of self, 15, 26, 98, 134
Chaos, 143, 177
Character, 64 – 68, 98, 100, 104
  flaws in, 16, 64, 86
  improvement of, 16, 22, 38, 40,
  41, 108
  measurement of, 13 – 15, 64,
  65 – 66, 67, 95
Charity, 42, 81
Charm, 62, 90, 130
Cheating, 13
Cheerfulness, 25, 28, 69, 152
Childhood, 26, 27, 28, 30, 36,
  54, 56, 58, 138, 159
Children, 20, 25, 27, 30, 49,
  52 – 60, 90, 123, 144, 151,
  174, 179, 190
  development of, 25, 26, 29, 53,
  57, 58
  love of, 47, 53, 54, 56, 59
  memories of, 32, 33, 55, 59
  play of, 27, 58, 158
  praise of, 16, 60

rearing of, 16, 54 – 55, 56,
  57 – 60
sleeping of, 57, 60, 151
teaching of, 57, 59, 60, 76
Choice, 69, 111, 141, 146, 149,
  160
Christmas, 20, 24, 186
Cigarettes, 45, 164
Cinema, 144, 185
Circumstances, 120, 167
Citizenship, 193, 198
Civilisation, 14, 56, 134, 138,
  141, 179, 186, 198, 202, 205
Civilisation's gift, 134 – 144
Class reunions, 31
Cleverness, 78, 96, 130
Clichés, 120
Clothes, 29, 68, 97, 98, 134, 141
Coldness, 81, 111, 122
Colds, 21, 137
Colour, 44, 73, 74, 116, 141,
  157, 174, 176
Comedy, comedians, 162, 196
Comfort, 15, 17, 23, 24, 97, 121
  128, 158, 165, 189
Commitment, 104, 194
Common sense, 85, 104, 118,
  129
Communication, 121, 122, 123,
  124
Community, 139, 180, 203
Companionship, 40
Company, 12, 37 – 40, 61
Compassion, 77, 93, 160
Competence, 196
Competition, 21, 113
Complaining, 84, 93, 14, 152
Complexity, 85
Compliments, 62, 90, 122
Compromise, 104
Compulsion, 90
Computers, 72, 89, 182
Concealment, 42
  of love, 45, 47
Concentration, 21, 77, 105
Condemnation, 84

Confession, 136
Confidence, 15
Conflict, 49, 79, 204, 205
Confrontation, 82
Conscience, 23 – 24
Consensus, 100, 193
Conservationists, 179
Consolation, 17, 42, 161
Constancy, 71, 91
Contemplation, 19
Contentment, 14, 27, 74, 158
Contests, 75
Contradictions, 30
Convenience, 71
Convention, 185
Conversation, 51, 65, 85, 88,
  120 – 132, 164
Conversion, 131
Convictions, 104, 105, 111, 128,
  154, 196
Coolness, 79, 81, 161
Correction, 42, 112, 147
Courage, 30, 73, 76 – 77, 107,
  114, 134, 152, 155, 172, 192
Courtesy, 60
Cowardice, 23, 76, 107
Creativity, 19, 74, 102, 136, 144
Credit, 76, 199
Cricket, 185
Crime, 72, 86
Crises, 49, 166
Criticism, 40, 43, 56, 84, 90, 93,
  130
Crying, 25, 36, 48, 69, 161
Culture, 134 – 144
Curiosity, 76, 136
Cynics, 68, 70, 74

D

Dancing, 23, 46, 74, 108, 140,
  141, 143, 151
Dangers, 108, 111, 112, 136,
  162, 187
Daring, 30, 102, 107, 108